BEING MESSY, BEING CHURCH

The Bible Reading Fellowship
15 The Chambers, Vineyard
Abingdon OX14 3FE
brf.org.uk

The Bible Reading Fellowship (BRF) is a Registered Charity (233280)

ISBN 978 0 85746 488 0
All rights reserved
First published 2017
10 9 8 7 6 5 4 3 2 1 0

Cover images © Lesley Cox; © Alison Thurlow; © Calvin Frans; © Marty Drake; © Mark Hird-Rutter; © Florence Jones; © James Pegg; © Kerstin Oderhem and © Jo Birkby

Acknowledgements
Unless otherwise stated, scripture quotations are taken from The Holy Bible, New International Version (Anglicised edition) copyright © 1979, 1984, 2011 by Biblica. Used by permission of Hodder & Stoughton Publishers, an Hachette UK company. All rights reserved. 'NIV' is a registered trademark of Biblica. UK trademark number 1448790.

Scripture quotations from The New Revised Standard Version of the Bible, Anglicised edition, copyright © 1989, 1995 by the Division of Christian Education of the National Council of the Churches of Christ in the United States of America. Used by permission. All rights reserved.

Every effort has been made to trace and contact copyright owners for material used in this resource. We apologise for any inadvertent omissions or errors, and would ask those concerned to contact us so that full acknowledgement can be made in the future.

A catalogue record for this book is available from the British Library

Printed and bound by CPI Group (UK) Ltd, Croydon CR0 4YY

BEING MESSY, BEING CHURCH

EXPLORING THE DIRECTION OF TRAVEL FOR TODAY'S CHURCH

EDITED BY IAN PAUL

CONTENTS

Foreword 7

Introduction: a church for all generations Ian Paul 11

MESSY DEVELOPMENTS

Messy Church in different contexts Karen Rooms 21

Messy teamwork: developing the faith of
team members Isabelle Hamley 37

Messy challenges: dangers and pitfalls Greg Ross 51

Making sacred spaces in Messy Church Jean Pienaar 65

Messy Church and the sacraments Philip North 79

MESSY IMPLICATIONS

Messy Church in a postmodern world Sabrina Müller 95

Messy Church and Sunday church in conversation Mark Rylands .. 107

Messy Church and play Judyth Roberts 121

The pastoral implications of Messy Church Irene Smale 131

Messy Church and evangelism Tim Sanderson 143

Messy Church and the challenge of
making disciples Stephen Kuhrt 155

Missional structures for missional outcomes Tim Dakin 169

Notes 189

FOREWORD

An email came round recently, from a member of the BRF marketing team, asking if we had a generic word to describe books like *Messy Church Theology*, *Messy Hospitality*, *Making Disciples in Messy Church* and *Messy Togetherness*. They said, 'The word we use in-house is *thinky* books, but we can't really use that in public...' Well, *Being Messy, Being Church* certainly fits into the series of 'thinky' books! We are deeply grateful to Ian and all the authors who have put so much thought into their fields over the years and have had the grace and skill to apply that thinking to Messy Church in such a generous and wise way, to help us all to think.

I came across a word this morning in the context of reading about the wisdom of God in Ephesians 3. The word is 'phronesis', a fine and noble-sounding word that one can pronounce with a slight elevation of the chin, as it feels so lofty and impressive. 'Today I shall set out to be phronetic,' we may chant as we get up each morning. It's the word Paul uses for insights that help us live out the wisdom of God in a practical way. I would offer the concept of phronesis to Messy Church team members as a happy attitude to have in mind as we read the collected wisdom and experience in these chapters. In other words, there's a lot of theory in these pages, and it's our job as Messy Church practitioners to let that exciting theory sift through our grounded, hands-on experience and, with the cooperation of the Holy Spirit, transform us and our actions.

Messy Church is firmly associated with practical wisdom: the outworking of discipleship; the living out of faith; and the mucky hands of disciples serving communities by washing up, sweeping up, peeling potatoes or creating works of art from the stuff of the earth and noxious explosions from chemicals. It is the applied wisdom of a lifetime of following Jesus, so that when we sit alongside a family, surrounded by planks of wood and screwdrivers, we know how to respond to the unexpected question about God—and we know how *not* to reply. After all, what would you say to an eight-year-old with autism who listens carefully to your introduction to the yoghurt-pot-based activity at Easter time, about Jesus' death and resurrection changing the world for ever, and then politely asks, '*Exactly how* did Jesus change the world for ever?'

The huge themes and questions dealt with in the chapters of this book will challenge our attitudes and ideas and encourage us to *do what we do* even better in our Messy Churches—to get on with the phronesis with renewed vision.

Sometimes it will be about reframing our whole attitude to what we're doing, maybe as we catch sight of the 'Modern Mainstream' from Sabrina Müller's chapter on the postmodern world in which we are Messy. We might catch a glimpse of the way we are doing evangelism—and could do it even better—from Tim Sanderson's chapter, or of discipleship as explored by Stephen Kuhrt.

Sometimes it will be about taking encouragement that equips us for the next stage of our work, by offering us ministry-validating phrases that nobody thinks to say to us in our home church. It is a huge encouragement, for example, to read Stephen Kuhrt's words of hope and purpose: 'Messy Church has used a potent combination of fun, craft, food and community to engage with children and their parents/carers and bring the love of God further into their lives.'

Sometimes it will be as if one of the writers opens a window to a new and energetic direction for our Messy ministry. Isabelle Hamley's chapter on building a team could do this, being a real eye-opener to the opportunities presented by a team for making disciples. Philip North is enthusiastic in urging us to make the most of the Eucharist. Irene Smale writes passionately about the pastoral possibilities inherent in a Messy Church.

Sometimes there will be an uncomfortable challenge to stop being satisfied with less than the best, as we find in the rigorous account of Karen Rooms' development of her Messy Church at St Ann's, with her great regard for listening and respect for local culture. There is also a challenge in Jean Pienaar's gentle and wise reflections on the different forms that 'space' takes in a Messy Church, or Judyth Roberts' reflections on the importance of play. Greg Ross's brave confrontation with the challenges of leading a Messy Church will also provide plenty of food for thought.

Sometimes there will be a call to those in strategic leadership to see the opportunities inherent in this movement, as we read in the chapter written by my own bishop, Tim Dakin, as he reflects on nodal leadership, and in Mark Rylands' chapter about the relationship of inherited and Messy Church.

Sometimes there will simply be a renewed understanding that God is behind it all, beneath it all, guiding it all and the goal of it all, an understanding that will reassure us of the higher purpose of those toilet roll innards and sock collections. As Mark Rylands writes, 'Messy Church, like Alpha, seems to be a movement inspired by God.'

Reading these chapters, I am struck by the changes that have happened since the teenage Messy Church was a baby, not that long ago. I'm struck by the thread of discipleship that runs through these chapters, with flashes of understanding, insight and experience not just from outside Messy Church but now coming from the inside as well. I'm struck by the international aspect of the Messy family, with contributors from Australia, South Africa and Switzerland as well as the UK. I'm struck by the fact that we are doing a little bit to even up the male/female balance in books of this sort, even if several of the female authors we approached weren't in a position to accept, so that it's still somewhat male-heavy compared with the glorious number of Messy female leaders.

More than anything, though, I am struck by the passion with which the writers share their ideas. This is no dry theological tome but a 'take me to the pub and argue over me' sort of book—a 'thinky' book indeed.

Thank you to everyone who has shared so generously, and thank you in advance to each Messy reader who has the humility and wisdom to put these ideas into practice in ways that make sense in their own community and church: go and be phronetic!

Lucy Moore, founder of Messy Church

INTRODUCTION: A CHURCH FOR ALL GENERATIONS

Revd Dr Ian Paul has wide experience in both pastoral ministry and theological education. With a background in studying mathematics and working in industrial business, he studied theology at Nottingham and completed a PhD in biblical interpretation. After ten years in ministry and another ten teaching theology, he now works freelance in teaching, ministry and writing. He is a member of the General Synod of the Church of England and the Archbishops' Council, and writes the widely read blog www.psephizo.com.

Facing the challenge

How would you characterise the challenges facing the church in the West? There is plenty of debate about the causes of our problems and what the solutions might be, but most commentators would agree in identifying the key issues.

The most obvious is the numerical decline in church attendance. My own denomination, the Church of England, now publishes annual attendance figures, which have shown steady decline for some years— but with some recent hints that, in certain areas, this trend might be on the turn. The church is not the only institution in the West to face such challenges; the rise of individualism and the loss in all areas of life of the value of institutional commitments has led to decline in membership of a whole range of organisations.[1] It is possible to argue that numbers attending are irrelevant; if church buildings are there, and clergy can serve as chaplains to their parishes, doesn't the business of (for example) the Church of England continue?[2] But if faith means anything, then numbers matter—because numbers represent people; and encounters with God in prayer and praise, in confession and listening, in word and sacrament, change people and equip them to change the world. The numbers are not simply a sign of fewer 'bums on seats' but of fewer people who have experienced a life-changing encounter with the living God.

A second, related concern is the rapid decline in the presence of children and young people in our churches. Recently I began to teach a class studying theology, and, as a matter of interest, I asked the group at what age they came to faith. Out of a group of 15, only two were not already committed Christians by the time they were 20 years old. Within a generation or two, we have moved from children's involvement in church or church-related activities being the norm to its being the exception. This has an impact not just on the present but on the future. In much of our communication with older people, including conversations about coming to and growing in faith, we draw on a shared cultural, intellectual and linguistic heritage, which relies on the experiences they had when they were younger. This is, and will be, less and less the case as we attempt to engage with successive generations who do not have a common vocabulary or set of ideas.

A third issue, which bridges the first two, is the question of discipleship. This is perhaps an area of greater debate: to what extent is discipleship a central idea in the New Testament? And how important is it in the life of our churches? It is worth noting here that the scriptures are not as fond as we are of using abstract nouns, and this should temper our search. But the Gospel writers appear to see the idea of being a disciple, sometimes expressed with reference to people and at other times expressed in the notion of 'following', as fairly central. The most explicit reference comes at the end of Matthew's Gospel, in the so-called 'great commission' of Matthew 28:19, 'Go and make disciples…'[3] But it is not offered as a novel idea, introduced at the last minute, so much as a summary of all that has happened in the preceding 27 chapters and the reason for their existence. Jesus ministered, taught and led his disciples so that they should then do the same for others—and not just for the 'lost sheep of the house of Israel' (Matthew 15:24, NRSV) but to the ends of the earth. It is no wonder, then, that Justin Welby, Archbishop of Canterbury, commented in his Lambeth Lecture on Evangelism:

> I want to start by saying just two simple sentences about the Church. First, the Church exists to worship God in Jesus Christ. Second, the Church exists to make new disciples of Jesus Christ. Everything else is decoration. Some of it may be very necessary, useful, or wonderful decoration—but it's decoration.[4]

Even though he does not use the language of 'discipleship' in the way the Gospels do, I think the apostle Paul would agree. His vision is that all who confess Christ as Lord, who have received the Spirit, should be built up until they are 'mature, attaining to the whole measure of the fullness of Christ' (Ephesians 4:13).

If numerical decline, loss of young people and the need to make disciples offer a challenge to the church, they are compounded by the rapid change in Western culture, which has opened up a chasm of communication between church and world. In the fragmenting culture of Western society, the church has, until very recently, occupied one narrow part of the spectrum. For many, the customs and culture that church people take for granted are quite alien to their everyday lives.[5]

What would we give, then, for a way of doing church that is drawing significant numbers of people, often those who have not had previous experience of church and belong to groups that traditional church does not reach? A way of doing church that is re-engaging with children and young people, and doing so in the context of worship and teaching for the whole family together? An approach that is encouraging discipleship not just in those who attend but also in the volunteers who are helping to run it? One that has a clear framework but is adaptable to a range of different contexts?

The offer of Messy Church

That appears to be what Messy Church is doing. In one particular outer estate area of Nottingham (where I live), traditional church has struggled to make an impact for decades, and it is acknowledged to be a tough area for ministry. And yet, since Messy Church has started there, it has drawn significant numbers and led to growth in the Sunday congregation as well. It has created a place for the sharing of faith and encounter with God for those who would never have darkened the doors of traditional church. A senior leader in the Church of England commented to me recently, 'I like the idea of Messy Church; I just don't like the name. How could "church" be "messy"?' Yet it is the down-to-earth reality of Messy Church and the radical hospitality echoing the incarnation that lowers the barriers to entry, bringing church closer to the people who need to discover it.

Messy Church started in the same year that the *Mission-shaped Church* report came to the General Synod of the Church of England, and, like many other fresh expressions of church, it seems to have met the mood of the moment. As a 'bottom-up' development by committed Christians in their local context, the way for recognition was cleared by the 'top-down' approval given by the report and its reception. Messy Church is not without its antecedents; its format has much in common with the holiday clubs run for many years by a variety of churches, and it shares the practice of making use of crafts and creativity while being intentional about the goal of sharing the good news of Jesus and growing disciples. Where it differs is in offering a context that is complete in itself (hence Messy *Church*), involving the whole family, rather than being both a contrast to and feed-in for a different way of doing church.

It is distinct, too, from other fresh expressions of church. The early involvement of The Bible Reading Fellowship in providing support and developing and disseminating resource materials has enabled Messy Church to be launched in a wide range of contexts, assisted by the combination of clarity of form and local flexibility (see the chapters in this book by Karen Rooms and Greg Ross). Its attitude to branding demonstrates this approach. Like the Alpha course, it has a brand and offers the use of branded materials: we live in a consumer culture that talks the language of brand identity. But, in contrast to Alpha, that brand identity can be adapted locally, provided that the key values of Messy Church are agreed. In focusing on values as much as form, it might be that Messy Church can avoid the difficulties of other movements (such as cell church and missional communities) where the form has been adopted without the commitment to values, meaning that these movements have not endured.

Questions and answers

The significance and growth of Messy Church raise important questions of ecclesiology, theology and mission. In terms of ecclesiology, where does Messy Church fit in relation to traditional forms and structures? This is not simply a question of organisation, nor merely a reflection of an obsession with order and control. Most commentators on the New Testament would agree that the early church did not simply have 'vertical' structures, with leadership, oversight and elders, but also key 'horizontal' structures, in terms of communication, sharing of resources and movement of apostolic ministry.[6] It is arguable that the Constantinian settlement, at the beginning of Christendom, removed this lateral missional dynamic, limiting ecclesiology to hierarchy alone. As Tim Dakin highlights in his chapter in this book, this dynamic has resurfaced at times of renewed missional activity, is needed today, and fundamentally changes the nature of episcopal leadership in enabling and encouraging the mission of the church.[7]

If the church is the place 'in which the pure Word of God is preached, and the Sacraments be duly ministered',[8] then the claim to be 'Messy Church' raises some unavoidable questions about practice, which perhaps were not in view when the movement was first started.[9] The most obvious is the question of baptism and Communion in Messy Church, and Philip North's engagement with this is vital. The practice of the sacraments raises further the issue of Messy Church's relationship with Sunday church (Mark Rylands), but also the challenge of Messy Church as a complete context for evangelism (Tim Sanderson), and the formation and growth of disciples (Stephen Kuhrt and Isabelle Hamley).

One of the most exciting dynamics of Messy Church is the rediscovery of the New Testament vision of whole-life discipleship and whole-life relationships within the community of faith and between this community and the world beyond faith. (One element of this, the communal meal, is also a hallmark of the success of the Alpha course.) I believe that this has a deep significance for engagement with our culture, which appears at the moment to be more divided than ever, but which is at the same time less and less tolerant of an approach to belief that compartmentalises different aspects of life. Since we are bodily-persons-in-community, there is a growing recognition of the importance of the physical reality of sacred space (Jean Pienaar) and the role of play in human development, growth and well-being (Judyth Roberts).

Looking to the future

These chapters do not answer all the questions, and to my mind there remain two outstanding challenges.

Sabrina Müller's fascinating exploration of Messy Church and its place within a sociological analysis of culture notes that most fresh expressions of church appeal to a specific cultural group under the mapping that she uses. The question, then, for all fresh expressions, and Messy Church with them, is: what should sit alongside and adjacent to Messy Church to engage with the groups for whom Messy Church is not the way into faith and discipleship?

The second major question is: how could or should Messy Church develop? If Messy Church provides an accessible place for families with young children and adults who are comfortable in this context, what might naturally come next as children make the transition into the teenage years?[10]

What is clear is that Messy Church is no passing fad and looks to become more established, not simply as a mission strategy but as a continuing expression of church in its own right. My hope and prayer is that the fascinating essays in this book will help both to consolidate that position and to provide resources and material for continued reflection for church leaders and practitioners in all their diversity of theological tradition and missional context.

MESSY DEVELOPMENTS

MESSY CHURCH IN DIFFERENT CONTEXTS

Revd Canon Karen Rooms is Canon Missioner of Leicester Cathedral and City Centre Transition Priest in the Leicester Holy Spirit parish. Prior to ordination she worked in industry and served as a mission partner with her family through Crosslinks in Tanzania for seven years. Since ordination she has worked in two inner-city parishes in Nottingham, has been Area Dean, and has been a founding member of the broad-based community-organising alliance Nottingham Citizens.

Thank you, Lucy Moore, for giving away Messy Church! In a world of copyright and patents, the permission to innovate that is offered with Messy Church is a grace and a gift. 'It's not meant to be a showcase-perfect model to be copied slavishly (heaven forbid), but an example to learn from.'[1] In the first instance, the model was offered with the expectation that it would be adapted. This is no surprise, given its emergence in the context of the Fresh Expressions movement that champions new ways of being church, where 'the emphasis is on starting something which is appropriate to its context, rather than cloning something that works elsewhere'.[2] The principle of adaptation is inherent in Messy Church.

In this chapter I will reflect on the adaptations we made with Messy Church on our five-year journey in an inner-city parish. I will draw on the work of missiologists engaged in issues of the gospel, culture and contextualisation, as well as a recent study of estates, class and culture by sociologist Dr Lisa McKenzie, based on her research in our parish. I will identify some of the particular tools, methods and questions we worked with to adapt our practice, and describe what we have been discovering and learning.

Starting

St Ann with Emmanuel Church is in a pedestrian precinct in the heart of a 1970s Wimpey estate on the edge of the city centre. The parish of Nottingham St Ann's is among the poorest two percent in the UK according to the Indices of Multiple Deprivation. The challenge to the church, with an ageing profile and 50% of its members travelling into the parish to worship, was to reconnect locally with five primary schools and a higher-than-average number of adults under 40 years old. The PCC wanted to develop its outreach to families and schools. We formed a delivery team and built relationships with those schools by offering Experience Christmas and Experience Easter,[3] and began to get a feel for the culture of the children in the parish. Then we committed to employing a part-time Children and Families Worker and to starting Messy Church.

Our aim was missional. It was about sharing the gospel, evangelism and building community. We aimed to develop a new worshipping community of children and families growing in Christian faith and discipleship, shaped by the values of our church, which inform all that we do. Those values are 'Experience God', 'Belong', 'Participate' and 'Journey out'. We were attentive to an equal focus on adults and children, aiming to facilitate sustained interaction between them. We wanted to make space for them to be creative and have fun. This was a 'technical' solution, employing an expert to fix the problem of no engagement with younger families in St Ann's, and it worked with the 'gap' model of change, bridging the gap between our existing profile and ministry and where we wanted to be.

As we began our journey, we also embarked on the congregational missional process Partnership for Missional Church, developed by Pat Keifert and Church Innovations.[4] Drawing on the language of Ronald A. Heifitz and Marty Linksy, Keifert describes mission, in our current context of fluid communities, relativism and consumerism, as an 'adaptive challenge'.[5] There is no quick fix. The church's problems (in our case, lack of younger families and poor engagement with our community) cannot be solved by authoritative expertise or standard operating procedures; rather, 'they require experiments, new discoveries and adjustments'.[6] This means failure, being consciously incompetent and learning from our mistakes. It also means that change is required of those who face the challenge—there is no rescuer, no off-the-shelf solution—and new ways need to be learnt. This challenged the way we initially thought of Messy Church as an 'answer' and a way to 'fix' these named problems. As we proceeded, Messy Church became less of an answer and more of a missional innovation, the container for our experimentation and learning in mission.

Our story: beginnings (year one)

It is after school on the last Monday of the month. Sixty under-11s, 18 parents and carers, and twelve church and Girl Guide volunteers are participating in a strictly timetabled and planned Messy Church. Chill (time with refreshments in the carpeted central section of our multipurpose building) is followed by Crafts, when the screens are opened to the hall. Celebration, an act of worship with two songs, a story and an interactive response, follows in the main church worship space. Finally, back in the hall, Chew, a sit-down hot meal, is served at family tables. Six families remember to come every month on that last Monday, love what they experience and invite their friends. One or two helpers—those who have the specific role of welcome—know their names.

There is a range of craft activities, and most tables, especially where there is food, are busy for the full 50 minutes or until the resources run out. The crafts are loosely tied to the biblically themed story, following the ideas in Lucy Moore's books. A helper who has prepared the activity hosts each table. One helper looks unhappy; the activity is attracting no one, after hours of home preparation. A handful of nine-year-old boys are playing football with one of the toddler pool balls, because making a glitter fish to link to the story later doesn't catch their attention or energy. It is an exercise in crowd control, especially during the worship, with toddlers exploring the enormous space of the church and the lovely carpeted sanctuary.

Later, only one or two church helpers sit at table with the families, and, before cakes and fruit can be served, many children are running around and playing with the toys they have found in the corner. The helpers are busying themselves serving, clearing up and tidying, having suggested that serving food at the hatch, cafeteria style, would make the process more efficient. They do not join in the worship because they are too busy clearing crafts and laying tables. There is an underlying model operating here—one of service providers and service users.

Over the summer holidays, with every good intention, the core team undertake to build on relationships and visit every family that has been to Messy Church more than twice in six months. The team members are met with suspicion and rarely does any form of meaningful conversation occur. Only a couple of visits lead to an invitation into the house. Only one family comes on the organised trip to the local country park.

Messy Christmas Eve is glorious. Baby Mia is held by her mother in our very own celebration of a new baby, and, as a teenager plays 'Little donkey' on the piano, children, parents and Sunday church members process round the church in costumes they have made earlier. Hands are sticky with glue and cookie mixture, and hearts are deeply grateful to be loved and together in this holy moment in their church. A two-year-old picks up the baby Jesus doll and kisses it in a simple act of adoration.

Our story: what has changed (year five)

Four years later, Messy Church continues on Mondays after school, but now it meets every fortnight. Sessions alternate between Messy Church (craft, worship, hot meal) and Messy Games (table-top games and craft, tuck shop, worship). We have a core membership of 12–15 semi-regular families at any given time, with five who have belonged to Messy Church since the beginning. We text everyone on our database on the morning of the days when we run a Messy event, to remind and invite them.

The crafts are set up by parents and church staff at a 9 o'clock Messy Breakfast on the morning of each event—a great time to catch up with all that has happened over the weekend in people's lives. Our sessions are fluid, with constant access to refreshments, crafts and games, and the craft activities include the ever-popular cooking table where puddings or biscuits are usually prepared. Crafts are, on the whole, 'unmanned' because those who set them up know what they are and can help others access them easily. There are simple laminated explanatory cards. We think of ourselves as being like shop assistants, noticing if there is interest in an activity and opening up the conversation: 'Shall we see what this is about?' Everyone pitches in to clear away.

Unless it is a special occasion like Christmas or a baptism, we worship in the round, in the smaller carpeted space, which offers better focus. A cross, Bible and candle are placed centrally to begin our worship time, and everyone knows the response: 'We welcome you.' We use symbols and repetition more, and words and screens less. I wonder if leaving the church worship space has helped us, as church staff, to leave Sunday church habits behind.

We still sit at table and eat together. With regular requests for our meal recipes, we offered weekly Messy dinner parties during Lent, where we prepared, cooked and then ate a three-course meal together. We used 'Table Talk for Messy Church', which everyone loved. The children read the conversational questions and we all took turns to answer. In response to the question 'If you could ask God for one thing, what would it be?' the children were open about their struggles in school and asked Jesus to help them. One parent asked God for a new house, knowing she was about to be evicted. The conversation turned naturally into prayer. Answers to prayer are celebrated in conversation, and new prayers made. The conversations at Messy Church are real and honest. One mum talked about her desire to increase her working hours, and another prayed aloud, there and then, for it to happen. God has answered prayers for sanctioned tax credits to be paid, and testimony has been offered round the dinner table.

There is a strong relational and participative feel to our gatherings and a conversational spirituality that voices the companionship of Jesus and presence of God in the everyday. A level of trust has developed between Sunday church and Messy Church people, and conversations are more honest. It feels completely different from the early days.

What is clear is that, over four years, Messy Church has changed, as have the parents, children and Sunday church helpers. What have we been learning about the relationship between St Ann's culture and the gospel? How has the change happened? What techniques have been used as we have adapted Messy Church in our particular context? How are we ourselves adapting and being changed, and how are those we are reaching out to adapting and being changed?

Culture

From mission studies exploring inculturation and the gospel, Aylward Shorter's definitions of culture are helpful. Culture means that 'everything that a human being thinks or does is an aspect of a pattern or whole… Culture controls their perceptions of reality. It offers them a system of meanings embodied in images and symbols. It shapes their understanding, feelings and behaviour. It gives them a group identity.'[7] It is 'a set of images, collectively inherited and experienced, that enable human beings to relate to one another in community and to the world in which they live, intellectually, emotionally, and behaviourally'.[8] In the context of the St Ann's parish, it is what sociologist Lisa McKenzie calls 'being St Ann's'. We are also aware that we have a distinctive church culture in which the gospel we announce is packaged.

'Being St Ann's'

St Ann's is an inner-city estate on the east side of Nottingham, the largest East Midlands city. The area was originally developed for a new proletariat workforce in the early 19th century. Much of its back-to-back terraced housing, very close to the centre of Nottingham, was still inhabited in the 1960s, and was in very poor condition before the area's redevelopment during the 1970s. The estate is a modernist project built by Wimpey to a 'Radburn' blueprint, and over half of its households are in social housing. Its labyrinthine layout is designed for a community without cars, perhaps because the working poor were not expected to have them. Despite the new housing, there are cultural continuities with the 'old' St Ann's.

St Ann's has always been the area where immigrant communities begin living in Nottingham. During the 19th century, the Scots, Welsh and Irish arrived and were followed by waves of Europeans and Irish after each of the 20th-century wars. More recently, the 'Windrush' migration from the Caribbean in the 1950s and 1960s has been followed by the 21st-century migrations of EU citizens and asylum seekers and refugees from war zones in Africa and the Middle East. Only 51% of St Ann's residents are white British, with 27% being African, Caribbean and mixed race, and the remaining 22% from Eastern Europe, the Middle East and Asia.

Since the 19th century, the area's history has been one of close-knit working communities, policing themselves through family affiliation and gangs, and this pattern continues to shape the estate today. Family life is very highly valued and motherhood is rated highly for women. While 45% of households with children are lone-parent households, extended families live within walking distance of each other. The families are as labyrinthine and complex as the estate architecture. It does not make economic sense for the fathers, brothers and boyfriends to live with their families. In her recent study of St Ann's, local sociologist Lisa McKenzie asked the question, 'Where are the men?'[9] She described them as 'passing by', in terms of being regularly in the house but not in a fixed or permanent way. St Ann's is characterised by multiple jobs per household, poverty wages and debt, together with poor health (obesity and mental health issues) and disability.

The low-cost housing in St Ann's means that it is a young community, with 41% aged between 20 and 44.[10] The area has five primary schools and one secondary school. Three-quarters of the children are eligible for free school meals and a high number have special needs or disabilities. While children do well at primary school, their academic achievements plummet at secondary level, with only seven percent securing five or more good GCSEs. This physical, social and economic environment provides the context for what might be described as a culture of poverty and a culture of 'getting by'.[11]

McKenzie explains the culture of 'getting by' as a 'knowledge' that 'comes in different forms, from where you can buy the cheapest chicken, to how you might handle the various government agencies you have to deal with'.[12] One day at Messy Church, an exhausted mum talked about her eviction earlier that day and about staying in a hotel with her children, waiting for a family hostel place. In the course of an hour and a half, four different women shared their own experiences of being homeless and living in the hostels, and offered her advice on where to get cheap food and how to deal with the agencies. Here was a strong informal social network of peers offering advice on 'getting by'.

Church culture

Before we started Messy Church, our parish church membership profile was very different from the younger profile of our social context, with two-thirds of the 70 regular worshippers being over 60 years old. I was appointed with the brief to develop our ministry and outreach in the schools and with children and families, following 32 years of consistent faithful ministry. The church had a middle-class culture, with 'doing things properly' as a controlling value, and intercessions revealed a high regard for law and order and public agencies. More congregation members lived outside the parish than inside, and one or two expressed real fear of the local community and of walking down the street.

The thick line separating the culture of the church from the culture of St Ann's is expressed physically at the entrance to the church. To enter the worship space, a person needs to pass vehicle prevention bollards, worshippers' parked cars obstructing the main entrance to the church, and three glass doors. It seems ironic that the only piece of art in the building is in the entrance area—a print of Holman Hunt's *Light of the World*, in which Jesus stands knocking on a closed door.

We adopted the strapline 'Believing in St Ann's' as an expression of who the worshipping community are, and as a challenge to worshippers to affirm the people of the parish. Within weeks of the strapline going on our church noticeboard, a local community group had a picture of it on their website. This underlined our sense of God's calling for us, which had been recognised and blessed by the community.

Inculturation

Starting Messy Church in the parish was an act of inculturation—offering Messy Church into this particular context. In doing so, we set up a dialectic between St Ann's culture and our church's middle-class culture, woven around the gospel we were giving witness to and sharing. Inculturation 'means the presentation and re-expression of the gospel in forms and terms proper to a culture—processes which result in the reinterpretation of both, without being unfaithful to either... Inculturation means both that the gospel challenges cultures, and that cultures re-express the gospel.'[13]

Missiologist Andrew Walls argues that two principles are held in tension in the encounter between the gospel and culture—the indigenising and the pilgrim. Following Christ's example of making himself at home in a particular culture in incarnation, indigenisation is about Christ making himself at home in different cultures, taking people as they are. Indigenising began with the decision made by the

Jewish elders in Acts 15 to allow Gentile believers to follow the Way inside their own culture, and Paul's letters continued to thrash out the cultural questions that ensued. Throughout history, Christianity has taken into itself the values and worldviews of particular situations and times. Seventh-century Irish Christianity looks very different from a 21st-century Nigerian expression of the faith.

What we learnt about the relationship between St Ann's culture and the gospel was that we needed to express the good news simply as the person of Christ. This approach began after one of the delivery team fed back a comment made by a mum to the planning meeting: 'I don't really know very much about Jesus.' Using the lectionary Gospel, we planned themes for a year under the heading 'Jesus is...' As a result, we were able to teach that Jesus is among us, in contrast to the 'absent male figures' of our culture, and we heard adults and children talk about Jesus using this language: 'Jesus is my friend'; 'Jesus is with me.' St Ann's helped us refocus on Jesus, away from our starting point with the theological frameworks and suggestions of the *Messy Church* books.

The 'pilgrim' principle challenges culture and takes the promise of transformation seriously; 'it whispers to [the believer] that he has no abiding city and warns him that to be faithful to Christ will put him out of step with his society'.[14] The gospel takes people on a journey of change which challenges culture.

In Messy Church terms, for families who were used to meals eaten on the sofa, to eat an evening meal together, sitting at a table, was countercultural. A communal meal with 'strangers' was even more of a cultural challenge. One mum would never eat in front of people outside her immediate family, so she got her children settled and then helped with serving and clearing away.

Stephen Kuhrt maps the joys and challenges of establishing what he calls 'Sssh-Free Church'.[15] We were particularly struck and challenged by the principle of 'allowing the expression of church to emerge from the culture of the newcomers rather than being imposed by existing members' and how 'the parents and children alone make the rules on how they should behave'.[16] Three key missional skills that are required by this approach are:

- attentive observation and understanding of culture
- deep listening to people
- willingness to change and let go of our ways of doing things

The mechanisms of adaptation

So how did we get from our anxious beginnings to where we are now? How has the change happened? What techniques, habits and practices have been used as we have adapted Messy Church in our particular context? How were we ourselves, and those we were working with, adapting and being changed?

Evaluation or reflective practice

From the very first session onward, we met one week later and evaluated the previous session as the starting place for planning the next. Sunday church volunteers attended this meeting predominantly, with one or occasionally two parents. The two questions we asked were, 'What went well?' and 'Even better if…?' This has become a discipline, a practice. The first question keeps us encouraged and focused on success. My experience is that the default for any group discussing or evaluating an event is to leap in immediately with what went wrong and what was difficult. This drains everyone. Recounting what went well is vital in maintaining motivation; when we let it slip, so does morale.

Initially, and understandably, turnout and logistics dominated the 'Even better if…' conversations as we came to terms with delivering the events. We weighed up possible solutions and then took action, trying something different each time until things worked better. Something changed for every session, and tweaking was regular practice. We asked parents in conversation about 'what worked well' and what would be 'even better if…' In the early days, we had games and toys available in the refreshments area where everyone gathered, before we opened up the craft area, partly driven by the fact that some helpers were not able to arrive on time. Now, the crafts (and games) are available from the start, with refreshments alongside throughout.

Our evaluation and planning meetings have taken different forms along the journey. When we introduced Messy Games and moved to fortnightly events, we held our Messy Church evaluation and planning meetings an hour before Messy Games, calling it Messy Cake and including more parents. This was a conscious move away from a 'service provider' mindset and a way to encourage wider participation (one of our core values). A third iteration (as already mentioned) is our Messy Breakfast at 9.00 am on the days of Messy Church and Messy Games, after parents have dropped their children to school. This is a time to eat and catch up on the weekend before setting up together; the planning is done beforehand by one person with those particular skills.

Our evaluations were also shaped by our aims and purpose. With some self-critique, we realised after six months that Messy Church would be 'even better if' more helpers got to know the families who came. We saw that in focusing on delivering an event *to* and *for* people (perhaps betraying our model of sharing the gospel and evangelism), we were neglecting to love our neighbours and build community *with* them. This evaluation against our aims and purpose led us to repentance, and we changed our behaviour to be intentional in making conversations and building friendships. We began asking a new evaluative question: 'Which relationships have been built?' As we responded to this question over the following year, we struggled until a colleague offered the insight that if you want to build community, you have to meet more than once a month.

Constant evaluation developed the team's attentiveness skills. We noticed bored boys and older children and included complex activities and 'boy' crafts, such as set-building for the story. When parents offered to help, we heard it as a real offer and not merely a compliment, and gave them roles immediately. We noticed that the huge church worship space was an invitation for exploration, so we moved worship to the central carpeted area; this in turn meant that we were worshipping in a space that belonged to everyone, not just 'the church', and levels of engagement went up.

Employing another evaluation tool, we prepared a simple set of questions to elicit feedback from helpers and families, both adults and children. We researched the appetite for a fortnightly Messy Church and asked about any change of shape that would be welcomed. Our evidence assured us that we had enough help to run the extra sessions, which would take a different shape—Messy Games. This more fluid format, in turn, later changed the way we did the Messy Church sessions.

Listening

Asking questions, listening and gathering feedback from helpers and families have been crucial tools for adaptation. We do this every 18 months and are often surprised as we hear why people come, what they enjoy, their ideas for 'Even better if...' and what they want to focus on in the worship time. After moving to a fortnightly event, we began to get feedback from parents such as 'I know people I would never have met otherwise. So I know people I meet in the street' and 'I enjoy helping the children and building relationships with you guys.' Using a questionnaire format in one-to-one conversations, people have been comfortable to say what they think, and to talk about Jesus and spiritual things, as well as suggesting practical changes. Texting people on the day of an event is really helpful in a non-diary culture.

Many people in St Ann's feel that they are looked down on and not really heard. There are endless consultations, but there is always a suspicion that the agenda has already been set elsewhere. So it was important to us not only to listen well but to engage with the ideas we received and make the changes that people suggested. We wanted to model the good news that there is a God who listens and who really hears our prayers. Our context meant that adapting Messy Church in this way made it intrinsically good news or 'gospel'.

One way we established a culture of listening in the team of helpers was through the practice of 'dwelling in the word'. This well-researched and tested method[17] is best described as a fusion of *lectio divina* and basic listening skills, and was introduced to the Sunday congregation through participation in Partnership for Missional Church. In our evaluation and planning meetings, the scripture for the theme or story was read slowly by one person, and we were invited to notice a phrase that caught our attention or a question that the text raised. After some silence, we worked in pairs, listening to a partner and asking them what they had noticed. Then roles were reversed, with the first speaker listening to their partner. This is not conversation; it is uninterrupted listening. Finally, each person shared with the group what they had heard their neighbour say—not what they themselves had noticed.

This practice has been embedded in our wider congregation over the years we have been running Messy Church, and it has made a significant impact. We are learning to listen to people who are different from us—who notice different things and have different opinions. It is a collaborative practice, making us less inclined to impose our views on others and more inclined to listen to the other in meetings. It is also a missional practice, making us better able to listen to those outside the church.

Using this practice enabled corporate listening to God in the helpers' team and a deeper sense of God as our Messy Church partner. As each person had a chance to speak and to be heard, there was heightened discernment about where God might be leading our focus for the next session. This caused a subtle but significant shift, as suggestions for change stemmed from spiritual discernment and not just pragmatic problem solving.

A further application of 'dwelling in the word' was as a way to tell the story during Messy worship—having the passage read, and then asking children and adults what they had noticed, or what questions they had, rather than telling them what to think. We began to learn to stop controlling the story, the gospel, and to trust others and God to do his work. We were all changed by listening to God in this way.

Conclusion

Messy Church in St Ann's has been a missional journey in a sailing boat, discerning and catching the wind of the Spirit's work in the world and culture of St Ann's. It has required self-knowledge and awareness, to recognise the particularities of who we are and of those to whom we are sent. We have constantly watched the weather, through listening to God and each other. We have habitually tacked, changed course and adapted our equipment to maximise our travel. We have jettisoned things that don't work and are no longer needed, and reshaped the boat to sail better in the waters of this culture. The hallmarks of our journey have been attentiveness, listening, responsiveness, experimentation, and letting go of ourselves and our own preferences.

Messy Church in our context began as a 'technical' fix, with target numbers and rigid expectations of outcomes and the way we would do things. It became an adaptive challenge alongside others with whom we were called to travel into a less prescribed future—a work which we believed to be God's and which constantly required faith, hope and love from us. We learned continually that it is not how well you run an event or offer hospitality that makes the difference; it is the quality of love and respect lived in relationship and community that really matters.

Further reading

Stephen B. Bevans, *Models of Contextual Theology* (Orbis, 2004)

Anthony J. Gittins, 'The universal in the local: power, piety and paradox in the formation of missionary community' in Stephen B. Bevans (ed.), *Mission and Culture: The Louis J. Luzbetak lectures* (Orbis, 2012), pp. 133–187

Stephen Kuhrt, *Church Growth through the Full Welcome of Children* (Grove, 2009)

Lisa McKenzie, *Getting By: Estates, class and culture in austerity Britain* (Policy Press, 2015)

Lucy Moore, *Messy Church: Fresh ideas for building a Christ-centred community* (BRF, 2006)

Aylward Shorter, 'Inculturation: win or lose the future?' in J.A. Scherer and S.B. Bevans (eds), *New Directions in Mission and Evangelism 3* (Faith and Culture) (Orbis, 1999), pp. 54–67

Aylward Shorter, 'Inculturation in Africa—the way forward' in Bevans (ed.), *Mission and Culture*, pp. 99–118

Andrew F. Walls, 'The gospel as prisoner and liberator of culture' in Scherer and Bevans (eds), *New Directions in Mission and Evangelism 3*, pp. 17–28

MESSY TEAMWORK: DEVELOPING THE FAITH OF TEAM MEMBERS

Isabelle Hamley is Chaplain to the Archbishop of Canterbury, having previously been Tutor in Biblical Studies at St John's School of Mission, Nottingham. Before ordination she worked as a lecturer and a probation officer. She discovered a passion for all-age worship and Messy Church during her curacy. She loves the Old Testament, chocolate and seeing people grow in faith.

One of the Messy Church mantras is that people need to be invited to know God in different ways—interactive ways and creative ways. Hence the wonderful displays of crafts, the games and the less-easy-to-categorise 'big mess' activities patiently prepared by teams of helpers. But crafts and activities on their own are only part of the story. At the heart of every craft is a helper, someone whose task on the day will be to talk, welcome, guide and, most importantly, share the story. The helper enables links to be made between what is being done and the big story we are a part of, the theme we are exploring on the day, the story of God and his people.

Messy Church isn't just practical; it is profoundly relational. Within this context, helpers are key. Their faith and their ability to draw people in, make links, facilitate sharing and 'talk faith' normally as part of informal human exchanges—all these rather complex mature skills are at the core of a successful Messy Church. By 'successful', I do not mean one that attracts hundreds but, rather, a Messy Church that helps attenders, young and old, to draw closer to Jesus—enabling discipleship rather than entertainment.

But let's consider our average congregation supporting a Messy Church initiative. In many churches, the very mention of 'sharing your faith' is enough to scare people under the pews or all the way up the bell tower. The thought of casually cutting out paper sheep while inviting others, of whatever age, to discuss religion is not something that most churchgoers would feel comfortable with. I have been part of many Messy Churches, as a parent, helper, trainee vicar, curate and vicar. I have also conducted an informal survey of other Messy Churches for this chapter—30 in all, from different church traditions, different socio-economic backgrounds and different configurations—and collated some responses in online forums. In most cases, advertising for much-needed volunteers (Messy Church is work-intensive) goes like this: 'Anyone can help! You can just do crafts, or welcome, or refreshments. You don't need a lot of knowledge or skills. It is an easy way to serve!' And in many ways, this is true. Messy Churches around the country are staffed by lovely, kind, committed, hardworking volunteers, some of whom find a way to contribute that they had never seen valued before. They are wonderful, and valuing these practical gifts is essential to being church and enabling the ministry of all believers.

When we advertise, coax, cajole or twist arms for volunteers, though, we rarely sell the job by saying, 'All you need to do is share your faith, help others to explore stories creatively, listen carefully to discern what God is already doing in a child's or parent's life, and respond.' Should we be more intentional in discerning who our helpers should be? Should we welcome all on the team, but work more closely to mentor and train? And what is the effect of serving on a Messy team on helpers themselves? Intentionality would involve developing strategy, not just for the place of Messy Church within the overall life of a local church but also for its organisation. Being strategic will inevitably bring out some of the tensions that underlie Messy Church. Is it really church? How do we make disciples? How do we order belonging, believing and behaving? What exactly are we trying to do? Working with these emerging tensions with a group of volunteers can be difficult, yet it can also be hugely creative and can foster unexpected depths of reflection and discipleship in the entire team.

The unexpected benefits of an open team

Most of the Messy Churches I have surveyed have an open-door policy for team members. A core team organises and plans the event, and large numbers of additional volunteers help on the day. Some volunteers might be highly enthusiastic; they may have seen Messy Church work elsewhere, have heard about it, or be desperate to see children come to church. Others are more tentative. In smaller, middle-of-the-road, traditional and often ageing congregations, it is usually a case of 'Let's see what the vicar's new idea is.'

In these contexts, something quite extraordinary can happen. Messy Church is not threatening. It does not usually replace a well-loved service. It does not try to change an existing service. It is just different—something else, something 'for them'—so volunteers who would baulk at guitars and glitter in a Sunday service are quite happy to accept it 'for the kids' on a Saturday or weekday. A door opens slightly on to a new world. New worship and new ways of doing things can be contemplated, if not fully approved of or considered as 'real church'.

In churches whose numbers have declined and age profiles have risen, there is often a feeling of despondency: 'Young people aren't interested in church. There is nothing you can do. Children just won't come. We've tried everything.' In one church, seeing 40 children from the local community come in for a first Messy Church was a revelation for many. Suddenly, the narrative of decline was challenged, and new hope was born. It was not necessarily comfortable hope, though. When churches tell themselves they have done everything, being proved wrong is not easy. Yet, at the same time, the inspiration of seeing something new can work wonders. An 'It's possible!' narrative can gradually start to supplant the despondency. The door opens further towards change, not just in new initiatives but in the original congregation.

There is no substitute for 'seeing with your own eyes' what God can do. Simply participating transforms the participants, and the transformation can be gently encouraged through judicious reflection with helpers—

reflecting on hospitality and what it means to meet others in a safe, non-demanding space; reflecting on culture and responding to difference; reflecting on the role of relationships and personal story sharing. In ways similar to the findings from the Weddings and Baptisms Project of the Church of England, we discover that when we create an open, non-judgemental environment, newcomers can express their own tentative spirituality in conversation with helpers. The helpers then need to listen out for the signs of God at work in these lives, and choose how to respond with an invitation to explore further.

Messy Church can provide the material for an exploration of what God is already doing in our communities, and how we may come alongside the existing work of the Spirit. But this requires attentiveness, skill and openness on the part of the helpers, which needs to be carefully nurtured by senior leaders, often over a long period of time.

Strategy and intentionality

While the mere fact of 'being present' accomplishes something, it is worth thinking about how to nurture and build a team intentionally. One of the best features of Messy Church is that it can enable churchgoers and non-churchgoers, established Christians, beginners and seekers, to contribute side-by-side. This is often touted as an ideal, but it needs strategy behind it to assist it to work smoothly and to make the most of the opportunities. It is worth asking ourselves what the role of different helpers is in terms of nurturing faith and facilitating worship in all the different parts of Messy Church, rather than dividing the roles between the sacred and the secular. When each helper is enabled to see their role as service to God, it can offer them a very new experience of being valued as ministers rather than just church attenders, and can help Christians to integrate their faith further with other parts of their lives.

The next question concerns the desirability of mixed teams of helpers. Should we only have people professing faith in charge of craft tables, for instance, so that they can adequately initiate discussions around the story? Should the core team, with spiritual leadership, involve those who are not sure of their faith or are simply exploring at this stage? The questions are best explored through the story of one specific Messy Church in Nottingham.

The organising team agreed that they would have a completely open approach to general help, and would proactively ask families who had attended regularly for about six months whether they would like to be involved in some aspect of helping. This was the outermost concentric circle. They then had a craft group, which met to prepare the practical details of the day. This was a smaller group, into which people were invited, and it was agreed that out of six to eight members, at least a couple of people should be from the 'fringe'—Messy Church attenders but not necessarily professing faith in the traditional sense. This was the mid-concentric circle. It also included church members who were not necessarily heavily involved in church but had caught a vision for working with families.

Finally there was a small core team of four or five who prayed, planned themes over the year and gave spiritual direction. Having a fringe member on this group was risky, but was really helpful in terms of keeping them in touch with the vast majority of attenders and seeing things from a completely different perspective. The fringe member's presence helped turn the core team inside out: it highlighted assumptions and prejudices, and challenged the type of 'closed group' mentality that creeps into even the best-intentioned groups. Care was taken to let this member know that their perspective was highly valued and that they were safe to speak up—and they often functioned as the truth-teller of the group.

It is worth pausing here for a minute, as this set-up for governance clearly departs from the well-established pattern of having more mature leaders in charge of all spiritual direction. Here we see an open pattern, with God firmly at the centre, with prayer and scripture as foundations, yet taking seriously the contribution of the 'other' who has not necessarily taken the steps of believing and behaving according to the traditional norms. Instead, they are invited to belong, invited into a creative dialogue that helps shape conversation with 'others like them'. It is an exercise in missional listening. In a culture where the role of the expert is increasingly disputed, and where hegemonic forms of authority are rejected, a collaborative approach comes across as less threatening. It also enables the church to grow organically rather than from the top down. Yet, as we will see later, it is not always a smooth journey.

To get back to our case study, the team worked proactively to enable interested people to take more responsibility, and came alongside them as they were introduced to the planning groups, who prayed and talked about faith much more deeply than in the Messy Church events themselves. The content of these small group meetings needed thinking through carefully, to ensure that newcomers would be welcomed as they were, yet without losing focus on what needed to be achieved, while enabling them to grow more comfortable with prayer and open discussion of faith. This was an intentional strategy towards discipling helpers—both those with a church background and those without. The core group came to function as a small group with a focus, starting with prayer, followed by a study on the theme for the next Messy Church, then a planning session. The strategy yielded interesting results, with fringe members becoming more committed and growing in faith, long-term church members growing in confidence and the ability to engage in 'God-talk', and main leaders growing in their ability to guide and mentor.

This approach is not without risks and surprises. As fringe members are drawn closer to the centre, they start to realise what discipleship means, and will often question whether this is the road they want to take. A core team member in the Nottingham Messy Church decided to leave because she realised that she did not want to engage in prayer or reading scripture; all she wanted from Messy Church was a nice experience and 'a good moral lesson' for her children. Stepping up her involvement helped her and the rest of the team to realise the gulf between what team members thought they were offering and what many attenders thought they were coming to.

The same strategy in a different context produced very different results: increased participation drew fringe members nearer but pushed core members out. Two initial members of the core team, who were used to running children's groups, found the concept of a free-flowing, discursive and interactive approach to faith and prayer impossible to handle. One found that talking about faith while doing crafts was 'too heavy', while the other struggled with letting participants write their own prayers as part of the activities, rather than leading from the front. The discipleship of these core members was challenged, as were methods of engaging in the wider church.

Long-term churchgoers can still find it challenging to talk about faith, God and Bible stories. Taking a strategic approach means that their ability can be developed gradually. This can be achieved by pairing less confident helpers with more confident ones at tables; by providing written material to help them (such as laminated cards on the table, making links between the crafts and story); and by spending time with the whole team in advance of the event, chatting about the theme. A helper recently remarked, 'I had never explained my faith to anyone before!' Messy Church had provided him with a major step forward in discipleship.

Nurturing volunteers to make Messy Church work means recognising the need for support, supervision and encouragement—with gentle mentoring, reminders to keep the focus on faith, and help in developing a language to talk about faith in personal terms (rather than as a set of propositions to agree with). Messy Church can be the theatre for incredible growth in discipleship among those who have attended church for many years already, yet not taken the step of being active witnesses. In many ways, Messy Church helps to expose gaps in discipleship and practice that are not challenged in 'traditional church'.

Support is needed for volunteers to grow in two less obvious areas. One is clarity about what Messy Church is trying to achieve in their particular context—is it a new congregation, an outreach or a 'halo' activity (something sitting alongside the main activities of the church)? This will shape what happens at the tables. The other is the need not to shy away from difficult things. It is easy to fall into the trap of tackling the easy, attention-grabbing stories of faith (Noah's ark, festivals and so on). If Messy Church is to be 'church' in any meaningful way, it needs to go beyond moral lessons or constantly upbeat messages, to embrace the whole message of scripture, the whole of life and the difficult call of the gospel.

Creating spaces that enable grieving and the processing of difficult emotions is more challenging. Even discussing such concepts can highlight some of the failures of traditional church to embrace the whole of human existence—another step in discipleship. Also, putting across the cost of discipleship is not easy or comfortable for helpers. It is easier to sell a highly pleasant, marketable product. Consciously looking at questions of discipleship reveals our own unease with the cost of following Christ, both for ourselves and for the way we articulate faith to others.

In many contexts, the helpers who experience the biggest impact of Messy Church seem to be those on the fringe, those loosely connected to church but fearful of traditional models. Messy Church offers them a way to belong first, to be accepted as they are, whatever stage of their journey they are at, and to ask questions and explore safely. A gardening club associated with one of my churches was asked to come and help make Easter gardens at Messy Church. Two years on, many of the club members who do not attend church are still helping regularly and enjoying it. Several of them have popped into services and have been open to discussing faith and spirituality. It is a long, slow journey, but one well worth making.

Tensions and questions

Although working with helpers is incredibly gratifying, listening to them and accepting their feedback inevitably highlights some of the tensions inherent in Messy Church, and its unavoidable limitations.

Some of these limitations are well known and apply beyond the issues concerning helpers. For example, what do you do when the children grow up? However much Messy Church tries to be 'all-age', few children keep coming beyond primary school, and parent helpers can then drop out too. At this point, it is time to take stock, realistically, of how far the Messy Church has fostered discipleship, and whether it is providing pathways for growth in faith amid changes in life circumstances. Unless other forms of being church are on offer and have been accessed by this point, it is easy for helpers simply to drift away.

Here we come face to face with the limitations of discipleship, unless something more than the Messy Church framework is made available. The very nature of Messy Church makes in-depth teaching difficult. If we want it to remain an outward-focused, easily accessible space, the stories and themes, however important, cannot reach the depth that is needed for long-term, whole-life discipleship. They can foster prayer and exploration and discussion, but these opportunities are limited in the main event, partly due to time restraints and partly due to noise levels and the need to attend to small children. While all-age spaces are vital, adults also need spaces for exploring faith differently.

In Messy Church, it is easy simply to recycle the 'good' stories and to capitalise on festivals. In addition, you cannot build on what has been done before without the risk of losing accessibility. There is tension in the question of what Messy Church is for in a particular context. With good groups of helpers, this issue can be highlighted and opened to discussion, which can lead to interesting reflections on the nature of discipleship and what is intended to happen through Messy Church. Taking a strategic, focused approach is once again the key to enabling helpers, as well as attenders, to grow. Encouraging them to think about the stories and running helpers' meetings as small groups can create the space to go deeper—although this comes with the risk of losing those who do not want to go beyond attendance at a single, one-format event. (In just the same way, it is difficult to foster discipleship solely through Sunday attendance.)

In addition, deeper reflection is limited by what is physically possible: Messy Church is time- and resource-intensive. It is rarely possible to run Messy Church more than once a month, and, when you do meet with helpers, much time has to be devoted to practical matters. Working together towards a goal is a good way towards developing discipleship. Drawing together and talking about our faith as we work is formative. The question is, is it enough? It is interesting that a third of the respondents to my survey of 30 Messy Churches identified discipleship as a problem they were 'working on'. We may want to ask, can church be church without discipleship? Do we need to take a different approach, considering that working in concentric circles has good biblical precedent? Jesus had an inner circle of three, then the Twelve, the 72, the 'disciples' and the crowds; different levels of mentoring and discipleship took place within these different contexts. Messy Church can replicate this model, particularly in work with helpers.

The most interesting aspect of working with varied groups of helpers is what it reveals about how Messy Church is perceived. Among more long-term churchgoers, there is a wide perception that Messy Church is not 'church' (highlighted by 90% of respondents to my survey). Many Messy Church leaders are working hard to change perceptions of what 'church' is. Interestingly, in a quick online poll of clergy, I found that most of them *would* see Messy Church as church and want attenders to see it as church, although a lot of 'traditional helpers' do not see it as such.

Of course, the underlying question that comes to the fore when these discussions happen is 'What is church?' Messy Church pushes the boundaries of traditional ecclesiology. Discussing it with helpers is fascinating, and can bring out all kinds of interesting angles and opportunities for deepening faith and understanding. With long-term churchgoers who struggle to see Messy Church as church, the question can foster helpful discussions on the nature of faith, the place of sacraments, what we mean by prayer, how we unpack scripture, and the place of community and relationships. The discussion can then be followed by strategic planning on what would enable a particular Messy Church to be 'church', and what the role of helpers in fostering worship, prayer and discipleship may be.

More interesting are the perceptions of those helpers drawn from 'the fringe', or those for whom Messy Church is their only form of church contact. A survey in a church where I worked unveiled some thought-provoking results. While leaders were committed to fostering Messy Church as 'church', fringe helpers struggled with the idea, which prompted us to dig more deeply into the perceptions of wider attenders. When asked whether attending Messy Church was 'coming to church', a good proportion said, 'Yes.' When unpacking this response through other questions, however, it became clear that, for most of these people, going to church meant going to the building or a church activity. If the question was phrased differently, using the words 'church service' or 'Christian worship', the answers were mostly 'No.' When asked what they valued or got out of Messy Church in terms of spirituality, the most frequent answers were 'Good moral stories to live by' and 'Something fun for the kids; we want them to be in contact with Christianity so that they can make their own decision.'

These responses are partly due to traditional (and often erroneous) concepts of what 'church' is, but not solely. The causes are also about self-perception and identity. A lot of the people we spoke to and surveyed did not see themselves as churchgoers; they did not necessarily see discipleship happening at Messy Church or want it to happen. They mostly had no intention of giving monetarily on a significant or regular basis; they did not want to be drawn in deeper or to make a time commitment to additional activities (such as a nurture group or Alpha course).

Involving some of these families in helping and planning led to two radically opposite effects. Some drew much closer in and started linking to other aspects of church as they observed faith more explicitly in the team. For them, Messy Church was a contact, a hub, where they met faith. From there, other involvement grew—small groups, community meetings, prayer and pastoral support—enabling them to take the next step on their journey of faith and give back to Messy Church through their own story. Others, however, backed right off as they felt uncomfortable with the fact that we prayed and believed, and specifically saw Messy Church as church and a place to deepen faith and commitment to God.

In some ways, this might be a good indicator of a Messy Church that *does* function as a discipling community; people around Jesus in the Gospels, and around the disciples in the early church, were sometimes drawn in, but many walked away, put off by the cost of discipleship. It also suggests that growing in discipleship involves more than the regular meeting with one big group (whether Messy Church or Sunday attendance); instead, growth happens when the initial experience feeds into a more focused, intimate, personal approach. Interestingly, in the 30 Messy Churches surveyed, all of those who reported growth in discipleship linked it to other activities arising out of Messy Church—whether helpers' groups, small study groups or other forms of involvement.

A subsidiary question raised by this experience is 'Can a group be "church" if there is no self-consciousness about it?' Speaking to leaders across many churches, I have often been told that people may not realise that Messy Church is church at first, but then they can be drawn in. Is this a fair incarnation of what scripture describes as a community of believers? Or do Messy Churches need to be more intentional and explicit about what they are (apart from just relying on the name to make it clear)? Conducting an honest survey of helpers and attenders can bring out some of the weak areas in what we do at Messy Church. This can be crucial in helping to shape programmes and sessions as well as a wider strategy for enabling a community to be formed around Jesus. More often than not, for this community to grow in depth, more will be needed than a monthly Messy Church, just as Sunday mornings cannot be the totality of 'church' in and of themselves.

Conclusion: the shape of church

Journeying with different Messy Churches in different contexts, and listening to others speak of their Messy Churches, I can be led to only one conclusion: there is no 'one size fits all'. Everywhere, however, reflecting with helpers and a leadership team is crucial in enabling honesty about what we are doing, as we decide on direction and set strategies for growth in depth and breadth. Working with mixed teams of helpers reveals considerable variation in understanding of and attitudes to Messy Church, and fascinating journeys into deeper discipleship. But it also shows that 'doing alongside' is not quite enough for developing discipleship. Simply helping and being part of a community does not necessarily yield discipleship, intentionality or commitment. In other words, belonging does not necessarily lead to believing. Not all are drawn deeper. If we are intentional about mentoring helpers and helping them grow in faith, it can easily lead them to decide that discipleship is not for them.

Inviting people to join a Messy Church team at different stages of faith is a powerful way to prompt everyone to assess where they are, what their presuppositions are, what they consider most important, and how they relate to the very concept of 'church'. For those on the helping team who come from non-church backgrounds, this can be their first experience of a small group that prays and seeks God, reads scripture and speaks a language of faith in everyday life. For those who are long-term churchgoers but have never really shared their faith or participated in small groups, it can be an opportunity for them to go beyond Sunday faith. For those who are much more used to church and groups, it is an opportunity to see God, faith and themselves as church through the eyes of others—with uncomfortable and stretching consequences. When led intentionally, helpers' meetings can function effectively as discipling spaces, paving the way to something else—a widening of the Messy Church community into an organic network of different groups, with space to both contribute and receive, space for faith to grow, and space for God to surprise us with a church much bigger than we could ever imagine.

MESSY CHALLENGES: DANGERS AND PITFALLS

Greg Ross is a Uniting Church Minister, based in Western Australia, having previously served as a Commissioned Youth Worker, an Aged Care Chaplain and a Minister of the Word. Greg grew up in a Christian home, his father being an ordained minister in the Methodist and then Uniting Church in Australia. He has been involved in leadership in church and community organisations in various capacities, and enjoys making music with community groups. He is married to Vicki and they have three adult children. In 2010, Greg and his team undertook a period of discernment to see if Messy Church was one of the ways in which they could engage with people not presently attending any church. Since then, St Augustine Messy Church in Bunbury has embraced a wide variety of people and connected them to Christ in a variety of messy ways. Greg is one of the Regional Coordinators for Messy Church in Western Australia.

Is Messy Church too messy?

One of the key challenges of running a Messy Church arises from people's reaction to the name of this gift of the Spirit. 'Messy Church', to many within the inherited church or those who have had a history with church, is a complete oxymoron. The idea that something called 'church' does not appear to happen 'decently and in order' (1 Corinthians 14:40, NRSV) is another sign that the church is one step closer to commencing a journey down the dangerously slippery slope to the dark side. But, as we shall see, this is not in fact the case.

Each Messy Church should have five foundational values:

1 It introduces people to the risen Christ…
2 by offering the unconditional hospitality of God…
3 in a way that has all ages sharing together in all parts of Messy Church…
4 and in ways that strive to engage people with creative opportunities and responses, and…
5 it celebrates the gift of the whole of life.

By adhering to these five values, Messy Church aims to be part of the *missio Dei* (mission of God) in transforming relationships and families of all shapes and sizes.

A careful explanation about these five foundational values of Messy Church, followed by a good practical demonstration of Messy Church, reveals that Messy Churches which remain faithful to these values are actually very highly structured and are founded on solid theological understandings. While Messy Church might appear to be the antithesis of 'proper church' to those who have only experienced an inherited form of church, everything that happens at a Messy Church does so 'decently and in order'. Perhaps the paraphrase of 1 Corinthians 14:39–40 in Eugene Peterson's *THE MESSAGE* gives a more helpful context to Messy Church: 'Three things, then, to sum this up: when you speak forth God's truth, speak your heart out. Don't tell people how they should or shouldn't pray when they're praying in tongues that you don't understand. Be courteous and considerate in everything.'

These foundational values have many things in common with the various forms of inherited church, and yet Messy Churches are distinctly different. We know this because those who come to Messy Church tell us again and again that it meets their need.

Many people who have grown up in and are comfortable with inherited forms of church are unable to see any reason why people wouldn't feel perfectly comfortable with the version of the Christian tradition that is practised in their patch. This 'push back' continues to present enormous challenges to lay leaders of Messy Church and the clergy who support and enable them. We have found that if some of those who are critical are specifically invited to come and experience Messy Church, it either quietens their concerns or transforms them into defenders of Messy Church.

Is it truly all-age?

A challenge for congregations embarking on or continuing to offer Messy Church to their communities is to keep all five values in tension and in equal view. It is easy to fall into the trap of focusing the crafts, songs, prayers, food and even the seating and language on little children, rather than ensuring that there is room and scope for all ages to be engaged and feel equally welcome. For example, some crafts have tended to attract mainly girls, and the crafts that are seen as easier to prepare are often those that appeal to people who are happy to colour, glue, stick and paint. These same crafts or activities do nothing at all to engage the demographic which is often missing from any church— males over the age of 12. The opportunity to create something from wood with real tools and lots of noise, or to be part of something that has an explosive outcome or tastes really good, takes a lot more time to prepare and often costs more. However, if these noisy, messy, time-consuming and more expensive activities might be the gifts that the Spirit of God uses to enter into a person's life in a new and fresh way, enabling them to revisit faith or even consider it for the first time, then we need to find ways to make them available.

One of the major reasons why Messy Church is proving to be so attractive, in so many different cultures around the world, is the difference it makes when teams deliberately hold tightly to these five foundational values. People tell us that they feel as though they can 'come as they are' to Messy Church. Given the frenetic pace at which many families live today, it is very important for them to get a chance to do something that doesn't involve being split up into age- or gender-based groups. Even some 'chronologically endowed' members of the community are thrilled to be allowed to do something messy in the confines of a church building. The engaging nature of the celebratory worship is another part of the attraction of Messy Church, and the provision of a meal is, in no small way, an introduction to an experience something like Jesus' Last Supper, where people share food and life around a meal and remember together the faith they are learning to participate in.

Is it led by a team?

A second challenge arises when a new Messy Church is envisioned, driven and controlled by one person, whether lay leader or clergy. The Messy Church can come to an early end in a context where the clergy person is moved after a short stay and the surrounding team has not been sufficiently invested in the Messy Church ministry, especially if the new clergy person is opposed to Messy Church, misinformed about it or simply not open to being involved. Where a Messy Church is the 'baby' of one key lay person, who is not sufficiently supported by clergy or the church governing body, burn-out often results. In other places, the key leader may hold so tightly to the reins that other willing team members withdraw, again bringing about the demise of the Messy Church.

Instead, it is necessary to identify suitably gifted leaders of all ages (from children to grandparents) for Messy Church, engage them in deepening their spirituality, give them training and build the team, so that each team member is familiar with the five key values and is able to keep them in clear focus. In a rapidly mobile world, there will always be changes in personnel, so the team always needs to be praying about and approaching new people to be incorporated.

A quite different challenge facing many Messy Church teams is that most of the leadership team might also be the leaders of the inherited model of church that stands alongside and supports this fresh expression of church. While we do not want to exclude supportive, committed and talented people from leadership, it is imperative that we do not exhaust their spiritual, emotional, financial and relational energy resources. Some congregations, which understand that they are running a 'mixed-economy' church, with an inherited and a fresh expression of church running in tandem, are able fully to support the release of leaders to focus on one or other of these expressions of church, without burdening them with guilt. In these churches, there is no sense of competition or jealousy but a common experience of being part of the mission of God in different but complementary ways. This is a goal that all of us can be aiming for.

One of the ongoing conversations that I have initiated with the inherited church congregation I serve involves telling and retelling the story of Messy Church and its foundational values. Our inherited form of church is now taking for granted that Messy Church (in its seventh year) is indeed 'church'. People are coming, baptisms are happening and Communion has taken place; people are giving money, becoming involved in some of the existing ministries of the congregation and leading us into brand new ministries. For the past two years, our church council has deliberately set a different time for our Annual Congregational Meeting, which traditionally followed the Sunday morning worship. The meeting is announced in such a way that all people from both the morning service and Messy Church are invited to take part, which clearly demonstrates that 'church' at St Augustine is bigger than just one or other of our worshipping communities. Along the way, I have constantly reminded those who attend the weekly Sunday morning service that it will take five years for those who come to the monthly Messy Church to say that they have attended 50 times.

Is it making disciples?

Another challenge that is regularly perceived by Messy Church teams (often as a thinly veiled criticism, hurled with some power at Messy Churches) is about whether or not Messy Church is making disciples. A response that Lucy Moore and the BRF Messy Church team have found useful is to lob back to the server's court the same question: can the inherited church demonstrate that it is making disciples? This approach levels the playing field to provide a fairer balance, and it encourages all forms of church to consider ways for faith to be experienced, shared, learned, formed and owned that are appropriate for each context.

The challenge of making disciples is not new for any form of church; the early church had to learn, relearn and constantly recontextualise the practice. This ever-evolving approach brought lots of conversation and evidently a great deal of criticism between different leaders and communities. To see this, we only have to read through the response that Paul wrote to the church in Corinth (in 1 Corinthians 9 and 10) or the discussions that Peter had with the Jerusalem Council in Acts 15.

For the last couple of hundred years, the church catholic has almost uniformly embraced various forms of education as its method of passing on the faith or discipling its members. While this may have been somewhat successful in earlier years, it clearly no longer works as it once did. The church's passion for educating the masses has released the masses from the prison of illiteracy and parochial superstition. Nice pat answers to thoughtful and often difficult questions, which once satisfied or silenced a teacher's class, will no longer be accepted as sufficient. Neither will inane platitudes delivered from a pulpit. Clearly, we need laity and clergy with a broad education who are well grounded in their own faith and are able to enter into open dialogue and discovery about the enormity of the divine mystery that we inadequately name as God. Sadly, a majority of the institutions charged with forming the leadership of churches continue to be decades behind the actual needs in the communities for which they are preparing our leaders (both lay and ordained).

We should not be at all surprised by the lack of response to tradition-ally accepted programmes and approaches to faith formation and discipleship, because they echo with the same hollow sound as many of our once-better-populated forms of inherited church, which have found that what they offer no longer serves to link the masses with their search for meaning and for connection with the divine. Several authors who are well experienced with a Messy Church approach have been researching and trialling various methods that provide an excellent warp (to use a weaving term) on which Messy Churches, in all their brilliant tapestry of difference, may weave a patterned weft for their own context. I highly recommend Paul Moore's book *Making Disciples in Messy Church* (BRF, 2013).

We need to develop an appropriately shaped discipleship journey for Messy Churches, because Messy Churches are attracting over half their membership from people who have little or no previous exposure to anything Christian at all. In Australia, the very earliest statistics collected from our 200 Messy Churches reveal that around 50% of those attending have no other connection with any Christian church. These statistics echo the much larger and more in-depth research of George Lings with Church Army in the UK. So teams running Messy Churches must never assume that the formational stories, prayers, music or sacramental life markers that shaped their faith development have ever been experienced by the majority of people attending their Messy Church.

Is it accessible?

Finding a way to invite people into the foundational and formational stories and experiences of the Christian faith in a fresh way is the core business of every Messy Church team. Every part of each Messy Church needs to be directed at offering a fresh and messy way for people to encounter the reality of God, who is at home with us in our mess. From the welcome to the choice of language, food, seating, activities, music and movement from one space to another, each part can be an invitation to experience something of the enormity and mystery of God. For our Messy Church team, Godly Play, with its thoughtful language, comfortable pace and invitation to use imagination and to respond with creativity, is without doubt a priceless gift.

We find it a great challenge to approach each Bible story without the blinkers of our past experience. The language of Godly Play gives us the freedom to do that, as shown in these words, which introduce the parable of the mustard seed:

> This box looks old. Parables are old. This box is the colour of gold. Parables are valuable, maybe even more valuable than gold. Look, the box has a lid. Boxes have lids and so do parables. Sometimes even if you are ready, you cannot enter the parable. The lid is like a door. Sometimes it is closed. If that happens, don't be discouraged. Come back to the parable again and again. One day it will open for you. The box looks like a present. Parables are presents. They were given to you before you were born. Even if you do not know what a parable is, it has still been given to you.[1]

When I am thinking about and praying and planning for Messy Church, I often like to exchange the word 'parable' from the paragraph above with the word 'faith'. The challenge for our team is to continue offering the present or gift of faith to all those who come to Messy Church in ways that enable them to open it and then own it for themselves—to remind them not to be discouraged on their adventure of faith, but to keep revisiting the gift given to them.

Is it connected with membership?

The visible and operational differences in the workings of church and the different understandings of what it means to be 'church', between inherited forms and fresh expressions like Messy Church, inevitably bring other challenges to Messy Church congregations. The issue of how people are recognised as 'members' is one that each denomination will have to address for themselves. It is vital that Messy Church leaders do not, for ease of process, simply default to the method for preparation and recognition of membership that they have traditionally used. A fresh approach, that holds to the five foundational values of Messy Church and meets the requirements of each denomination, needs to be developed for each context. An honest and open review after a membership journey, that leads to adaptation and further evolution, is also essential for the future growth of each Messy Church.

The next consequential hurdle that many Messy Churches face, once they have shared in a 'Messy membership' process, is about how congregations adapt their meetings and processes to offer the same kind of hospitable welcome that people experience at Messy Church. The games and tactics that are played out in almost every inherited form of church I have seen will not enrich people's faith. In fact, the opposite may be true. If churches are committed to growing disciples and extending the welcome of Christ, then the way many of us meet together to make decisions will need to be reimagined and reframed.

Understanding patterns of attendance (if they can be found in Messy Church) is another challenge that those who are planning and preparing Messy Church services face each time they are held. In Australia, the pattern of church attendance within inherited forms of church, revealed in the National Church Life Survey, has been telling us for some years that people who attend church every week are in the minority. The McCrindle research company released this information in time for Easter 2013 (www.mccrindle.com.au), based on the 2011 Australian National Census.

Australia has more churches (13,000) than schools (9500), and more Australians attend a church service each week (1.8 million) than there are people in South Australia (1.6 million).

And while the latest census results show that Christianity is the religion with which most Australians identify (61.1%), well above the second most popular religion in Australia, Buddhism (2.5%), less than one in seven of the Australians who ticked 'Christianity' on their census form regularly attend a church.

Easter is a time of the year when church attendance increases, but what do the 92% of Australians who are not regular church attendees think of churches, and churchgoing, in 2013?

- 47% responded that 'church is irrelevant to my life'.
- 26% responded that 'they don't accept how [Christianity] is taught'.
- 24% responded that '[church] has an outdated style'.
- 22% responded that they have 'issues with clergy/ministers'.
- 19% responded that they 'don't believe the Bible'.
- 18% responded that they are 'too busy to attend'.

This definitive, publicly sourced data only heightens the need for the church catholic to engage openly in fresh ways of sharing the gift of faith—and the need for fresh expressions of church that do what Jesus did in meeting and accepting people just as they are, which is one of the key values of Messy Church. This does not mean that we have to abandon the inherited form of church completely. But it does mean that Messy Churches need to be constantly vigilant that they do not start appearing, to the communities that they are attracting and welcoming, the way that inherited forms of church appear to the majority of Australians today. This data also highlights the need for the church catholic truly to embrace the way of being 'church' that was identified by the former Archbishop of Canterbury Rowan Williams as 'a mixed-economy church' where both inherited and fresh expressions of church exist together and are equally valued as integral to the whole mission of God.

Is it sacramental?

In Messy Churches that are led by committed and talented lay leaders, the issue of the place and administration of the sacraments can often be a point of challenge, depending on denominational rulings and the flexibility and support of any clergy in placement.[2] As identified above, denominations and congregations will need to approach the administration of any sacraments in a fresh and deliberately 'Messy Church' way. Over the seven years of our Messy Church's life, we have had several baptisms of primary-school-aged children and some parents who have responded to the sharing of the meaning and purpose of baptism through the use of the Godly Play curriculum. For each one, this has been the point they identify as the time when they really 'belonged'. One family had to move away for a couple of years due to work, and when they returned to Messy Church for the first time, they entered the church building announcing, 'We're home!'

For those who have grown up with little or no exposure to church, or without any experience of a traditional eucharistic liturgy, the image of 'body and blood' is a major hurdle; for many, it is a chasm too wide to be bridged, particularly given the rise of vegetarianism across the Western world. Again, in our context, the gift of Godly Play has enabled us to share the 'feast of the good shepherd' in a way that includes all those who choose to accept the invitation, with a life-changing outcome. One parent who grew up in one of the major Christian denominations commented to me after our first Holy Communion, 'That was fantastic! We've built and are now all part of a wonderful community!'

Developing appropriately worded, theologically sound and suitably accessible liturgies for sacraments in any denomination is an important work if Messy Churches are truly to be 'church' in every way. Gaining approval for the administration of sacraments by suitably trained laypeople, or for the use of 'reserved sacraments', may be one way in which these gifts of grace can be shared in ways previously unimagined. I can hear an echo of the argument that Peter and the Council in Jerusalem had all those years ago, when he met and ate with and baptised those on whom the Spirit had fallen, without the permission of the Council.

Is it worth the effort?

The final challenge is one that almost every Messy Church or fresh expression of church has faced from their sisters and brothers who are part of the inherited form of church: 'So when are the people from Messy Church going to come to morning [that is, 'proper'] church?' Only recently I encountered a newly ordained clergyperson who had been told during formation in theological college that Messy Church was a bridge to proper church.

From the beginning, Messy Church has been seen by its founders as 'church in its own right'. Messy Church, when adhering to its five foundational values, is for those who are outside the inherited church. Messy Church is a recognition that inherited church, while valued by those who attend, was not the warp of thread on which the particular people who come to Messy Churches were willing to see themselves woven. In its 13 years of existence, Messy Church has added significantly to the brilliantly colourful and wildly patterned tapestry of the whole church catholic. It is in every way a 'gift of the Spirit', to use the words of Archbishop Justin Welby in his address to the recent International Messy Church Conference in May 2016:

> I ought to be surrounded by all the paraphernalia and the life and buzz that I find in any church that is engaged in Messy Church. There's just a sense of stuff happening, the Holy Spirit happening, God happening, and best of all it's not happening in a straitjacketed way, but in flexible and imaginative ways.

> We talk a lot about the need to pass on the gospel afresh in each generation, and the trouble with that is it sounds a bit linear, a bit like standing in a queue. The trouble with that is, most of us aren't very good at queues. We do queues—at least, I do queues, because I'm English, and invariably I'm seething at the person in front of the queue who is doing something very complicated.

> Messy Church breaks all the queuing down and turns things into a circle. It's a circle of all ages meeting together to engage in who God is, in a way that works for them. When you say it, it is so obvious, and yet you've started. It is genius and insight and wonderful and a gift of the Spirit. We need to be church where everyone feels they are a part of it—that everyone comes in and can discover God, discover who Jesus is, be reached out to, to

engage with him. This is not church for children! It is church for church! It's church for everyone! And that's why I want to encourage you to be pushing out the boundaries, being flexible, being imaginative, being a circle of love that joins people with Christ at the centre. I want to encourage you never to be bound by 'the way we've always done it' but constantly to be looking, as you become more international, [at] what you learn from each other, [at] how you represent in Messy Church this extraordinary thing which is the global church.

You are a gift to the church. You've set churches and parishes on journeys they never thought they could make in a million years, and somehow you've enabled them to have the confidence to do it.

With support like Archbishop Justin's for Messy Churches, and the worldwide sharing of Messy resources, friendships, prayers and more, the challenges facing Messy Churches can be transformed into opportunities. We can look forward to seeing the surprisingly messy ways in which the Spirit will move us next.

MAKING SACRED SPACES IN MESSY CHURCH

Jean Pienaar initiated the first South African Messy Church in December 2009, in suburban Johannesburg, and is one of the Regional Coordinators for Messy Church in South Africa. She lives in Johannesburg with her husband and three active sons.

Traditionally, sacred space is regarded as space that is 'set apart', classically represented by a church building with lofty architecture, ornate interiors and signage indicating the need for respect ('Silence, please', 'No mobile phones' and so on).

Sacred space is far more than built form, however. Sacred space is where we can expect to encounter and worship God. Yet our understanding or perception of God also shapes the sacred spaces that we create. Theology informs architecture and the use of space. Tall ceilings may indicate a God who is relatively far away; the need for quietness suggests a God who demands absolute obedience. If our understanding is that God is accessible, creative, playful and embracing, what might the sacred space we create look like?

Messy Church might use different spaces within its multiple different contexts—in a church, school or community hall, or in a public facility such as a park. How do we ensure that sacred space is created there, such that it is possible to facilitate encounter with God?

Understanding the sacred

In order to discuss ways to create sacred space in Messy Church, it is important first to explore the definition of 'sacred' and then to understand the different facets of sacred space.

Theologians have tended towards inclusive understandings of the term 'sacred'. Ignatian spirituality is based on an understanding that God is active, personal and present. As such, God can be found everywhere. Like St Ignatius of Loyola, Pierre Teilhard de Chardin (1881–1955) believed that religion could not be separated from life in general.[1] Everything, then, has the potential to be sacred.

In contrast to the theologians, philosophers such as Emile Durkheim (1858–1917) and Mircea Eliade (1907–86) have wrestled with the definition of 'sacred' to a greater extent, particularly in distinguishing between the sacred and the profane.[2] Messy Church often operates at the junction between sacred and profane in terms of the space where it happens and the people who attend. In Eliade's view, religion uses aspects of the empirical world to create meaning, images and symbols that reflect the essence of the sacred.[3] For Durkheim, however, once profane objects are understood to be sacred, they become symbols of religious beliefs, sentiments and practices.[4] In effect, then, the profane can become sacred through intensive interpretation.

It is not surprising that the definition of 'sacred' informs the understanding of sacred space. Based on Ignatius' understanding of God as being everywhere, sacred space is not in a particular building or landscape; rather, the potential for sacred space is everywhere.

For Martin Heidegger (1889–1976), any place where a person might exist has the potential to be spiritual or sacred.[5] This speaks to the temporality of sacred space and the role of a human being or community of people in making space sacred. The vertical, experiential component of space (the sacred) contrasts with the scientifically defined, horizontal understanding of space.[6] As such, sacred space is not necessarily tied to a particular building or piece of land that has been consecrated, but is a place where God is encountered at a particular time.

This sentiment is echoed by Michel Foucault (1926–84), who asserts that sacred space is integral to and inherent within all space.[7] Foucault coined the term 'heterotopia', which he described as a place of 'otherness' which can evolve in function over time. Heterotopias are isolated, yet penetrable. For Foucault, sacred spaces have the potential to be heterotopias, especially in terms of the relational and emotional spaces they embrace as they facilitate opportunity for worship and encounter with God.

The functions of sacred space

Because of this, it is clear that while sacred space may be everywhere, humans acquire a sense of the sacred from the places that are familiar to them. It is also clear that sacred space does not need to be limited to history or architecture, but is as relevant today as it was in ancient times. The sacred can provide an unconscious sense of heterotopia, an 'otherness' within the mundane that is not necessarily tangible. In terms of Heidegger's vertical connectedness, sacred space can provide a place for worship and replenishment.

Arguably, sacred space can also provide a unifying and healing element within the community. This speaks to the importance of Heidegger's horizontal connectedness (between people and the environment) of the physical and scientific space. Historically, sacred space provided a place of safety and trust, since it was identified with those who were moral guardians and helpers of the poor and needy. In a world of vast inequalities, sacred space can and often does still fulfil this practical and important role.

The study of the influence of space on human well-being, although once regarded within the esoterical realm, now has a professional register of consultants.[8] In her book *Children's Spirituality* Rebecca Nye argues that many Christians have a strong attachment to a familiar or significant place that helps or has helped them encounter God.[9] This place then becomes a sanctuary—a holy and safe place. A sacred space that is both holy and safe would support an encounter with God.

Nye also explains the differences between physical space, emotional space and auditory space, which evoke different aspects of encounter.

- **Physical space** is created through architecture and built form. From a physical perspective, sacred space is often decorated with art and artefacts that express the theology of God's nature.[10] The Sistine Chapel within St Peter's Basilica in Vatican City illustrates the deliberate way in which sacred space is decorated and reflects the historical perceptions of God within that place. Specific attention is often given to the threshold or entrance to the sacred space, through the use of doors, archways or colonnades. The presence of a distinctive threshold reinforces the sense that the sacred space is distinct from the profane.

- **Emotional space** includes the space to be apart, or to be ourselves with our own distinct opinions. It also includes the space where we can feel closely held and safe.[11] As we have noted, safety and trust are significant considerations in creating sacred space, especially if that space is to facilitate encounter with God.

- **Auditory space**, on the other hand, provides the space for spiritual conversations. Nye emphasises the importance of silence and unrushed time when the conversations can take place, either actually or figuratively, the latter when an issue is so important that it can't adequately be put into words.[12]

It is clear, then, that each sacred space embodies elements of physical space, emotional space and auditory space. In the Messy Church context, physical space is contextual and there might be severe limitations in its organisation, particularly in terms of the existing architecture. Whatever space is available, it is important to be conscious of creating a safe space that accommodates silences, that welcomes deep conversations, and that embraces joy, wonder, frustration and hurt—space that meets people where they are.

Seven sacred spaces

In order to explore the sacred spaces within churches, George Lings turns to the common spaces within monastic communities, both ancient and contemporary, as they search for greater spiritual clarity and authentic humanity, living as salt and light in the world.[13] Lings identifies seven sacred spaces that enable different types of encounter with God and with other members of the community. He argues that each of these spaces plays a distinct role, and he therefore recommends that each space should be present within a church community, to promote the sustainability and health of the community and their personal and communal relationship with God.

- **Cell:** The cell is the equivalent of the bedroom, a dedicated quiet corner that facilitates time alone with God in silence and stillness.[14] Contemplatives understand the need for this type of time and space. Henri Nouwen explained that 'solitude is the furnace of transformation'.[15] Quiet, reflective time is essential for listening to God and for personal growth.

- **Chapel:** In contrast to the cell, the chapel is the place of public and corporate worship, characterised by ritual, liturgy and sacraments. While chapel is important, Lings emphasises that church should constitute more than just chapel, especially if it is working with the other six sacred spaces.[16]

- **Chapter:** Chapter represents the space of communication, corporate discussion, debate, disagreement and intentional accountability.[17] It is the place of decision making and should therefore be characterised by tolerance and humility, even though differences of opinion are to be expected.

- **Cloister:** The cloisters are the pathways and spaces that connect the intentional spaces, and represent places of relaxation. The cloister offers temporary relief from community, as well as allowing for unplanned meetings and conversations.[18]

- **Garden:** Within monastic communities, the garden represents the place of manual work and productivity, as the produce provides sustenance and income and allows for self-sufficiency. The garden is regarded as a place of service and provision for the community.[19] In many respects, the garden is the link with the 'outside world', the natural world, which feeds the body and soul.

- **Refectory:** The refectory is the place of preparing and eating food for physical nourishment. However, rather than just mechanically filling stomachs, it is also the place where community is nurtured through conversation, silence and hospitality. The refectory performs an important role in terms of the informal socialisation of new members.[20]

- **Scriptorium:** Originally designated as the space where scripture was studied and meticulously copied, the scriptorium represents the library of the community—not a dusty bookcase of second-hand books, but rather the place of study, research and discovery.[21]

By applying the ancient language of the monastics to different contexts, it is evident that different communities tend to have similar essences but different shapes or forms as a result of their particular environment and situation. For Lings, the seven sacred spaces connect with what it is to be human, illustrating that healthy individuals and healthy communities need to be both alone and together.[22] Each of the seven spaces provides opportunity for growth in the classic virtues. It is sobering to realise that merely doing chapel better (the focus of many churches) will not necessarily promote healthy and holistic communities.

Sacred spaces within Messy Church values

If Messy Church is church, and is serious about building communities and facilitating their search for spiritual clarity and more authentic humanity, it is worth exploring how these seven sacred spaces fit into

Messy Church. The Messy Church values of creativity, celebration and hospitality encompass different types of activities within a typical Messy Church programme, while the values of being all-age and Christ-centredness are relevant to all parts of Messy Church. The sections below explore each Messy Church value and the sacred space(s) that it embraces.

Creativity

The time for creativity generally involves a number of different activities that will appeal to the families that are attending, depending on facilities and resources available. By being conscious of the various styles of learning, the value of creativity links with the sacred spaces of the cell, the scriptorium, the cloister and possibly the garden, which facilitate personal learning, discovery and relationship-building.

In fact, the historical link between art (the creative process) and religion is worth noting. From the beginning of human history, art has been synonymous with the themes and interpretations of religious concepts, and has been a vehicle for connection with the transcendent. Since art transmits the beliefs and values of a culture, it often has strong religious or spiritual dimensions. Therefore, the mere process of engaging in creative activities can facilitate encounter with God. Space needs to facilitate the creative process.

The Messy Church value of creativity tends to be played out in small groups, around tables or on the floor. The discussion question linked to each activity provides a platform for further discovery and connection. The creative small groups provide the context for personal and group learning, but they also accommodate unintentional meetings, chance encounters and conversations, in a similar way to the cloister. Creative activities therefore play a much more significant role than the obvious entertaining and educating.

Creative activities should also include quiet, prayerful spaces that reflect the silence of the cell, allowing personal reflection and deep listening to God. It is important that those who attend Messy Church learn how to make quiet spaces within their homes and other familiar environments.

If at all feasible, activities that recognise and connect with the natural environment and the Creator should embrace the sacred space of the garden. The garden is also reflected in service to the community, where 'real-life issues' are held and not judged.

In essence, then, the time of creativity is deeply spiritual in its role of building community and providing an opportunity for personal growth. The actual activities may capture the imaginations of those attending but are largely incidental in encouraging people to encounter God.

Celebration

Celebration is the time of corporate worship, often involving some form of simple ritual (song, story and prayer). This value of Messy Church is the most obvious expression of the sacred space of the chapel. In certain contexts, though not all, the time of celebration occurs within the church building where Sunday worship happens. The advantages of this are that it provides a welcoming link to the broader church environment and creates familiarity, along with a sense of mystery.

For one of the Messy Church families in Johannesburg, Messy Church was a way for the young children to learn to enjoy church. Previously, some children had been petrified by the seating arrangements, which they had associated with watching the dramatisation of a 'scary' fairytale, so their families had avoided church. Having experienced the celebration component in a relaxed environment within the church building, the children are no longer afraid of coming into a church building.

However, not all Messy Churches will exist within the grounds of established churches, and for good reason. In this context, the celebration component of Messy Church should still allow for ritual, liturgy and sacraments, even if they operate on a simplified basis.[23] As George Lings mentions, chapels don't need to be grand, especially if they are working with the other six sacred spaces, but they do need to be evocative.[24] It is therefore advisable to use a space that is away from the distractions of the craft activities or the temptations of the meal, where those who are attending Messy Church can corporately and publicly celebrate their encounter with God.

Hospitality

Based on the example set by Jesus, hospitality nearly always involves food and liquid refreshment, and ultimately builds community. Jesus' circle of meal companions extended beyond the disciples to include the tax collectors and 'sinners'—the despised people in society. Messy Church meals should be similarly inclusive.

Shared meals are spaces for conversation and sharing, together with physical nourishment. With the pressurised work schedule of parents and the increasing trend towards TV dinners, fewer families than ever sit together around a table for even one meal per day.

Although the value of hospitality is most closely linked with the refectory, the space for food, emotional and spiritual nourishment is not limited to the meal time. The value of hospitality should extend to the nature of the welcome and a non-judgemental attitude towards the visitors and explorers within the other sacred spaces of Messy Church. Just as this value is not confined to the refectory, so the informal conversations that might be expected in the cloister can also happen around the meal table.

All-age

The all-age value of Messy Church is difficult to assign to any particular space, perhaps because it encompasses inclusivity in respect of many other dimensions besides age. Fundamentally, the all-age value speaks to the inclusivity of people, irrespective of their background; it speaks of a diverse yet unified God.[25] All-age is emphasised within the theme of inclusivity because, historically, traditional church has divided people up on the basis of age.

All-age is such a key value that it infiltrates all the spaces, from 'chapter', where the decisions regarding the different craft activities are made, to 'chapel', the communal celebration that is planned for readers and non-readers alike, and 'refectory', involving food for fussy eaters or those who find it difficult to cut with a knife or chew. All-age should be a mentality that pervades all the spaces of Messy Church. The inclusive notion of all-age and the opportunities for joint learning and teaching are sacred in themselves.

Christ-centredness

Like the Messy Church value of all-age, being Christ-centred permeates all other spaces and activities. Christ-centredness distinguishes Messy Church from other activities, clubs or gatherings and is the keystone for the other values that form part of Messy Church. Christ-centredness should inform the decisions that are made and deliberations that take place (chapter). The Christian message should also be central to the craft activities (encompassing the cell, scriptorium, cloister and garden), the celebration (chapel) and the meal (refectory). The value of Christ-centredness should also infiltrate the homes and 'gardens' of those who have been involved, spilling over into their manual work and productivity.

As we have seen, the seven sacred spaces that are common to ancient and contemporary monastic communities are inherent within the values of Messy Church. If the spaces within Messy Church are created and used properly, it is likely that the gathered community will find greater spiritual clarity and learn a more authentic humanity as they build relationships with one another and encounter God.

Consciously making sacred space

The physical presence of a church building might or might not conjure up a sense of sacred space for the families who attend Messy Church. Whether or not a consecrated building is used, what are the key lessons for making sacred space, not just a holy mess?

- Building community is essential to the creation of sacred space. In this regard, the architecture of the building that is used might be immaterial in creating sacred space. Sacred space is created where community is built; consciously building community creates sacred space. Once community leaves the space, is it still sacred?

- Sacred space has a temporality—a time dimension. This being the case, the sacred space will be unique to each community gathered. For example, a particular tree or symbol that is regarded as sacred to one community may not be considered sacred for another community that meets there on a different occasion. In places that are not specifically regarded as sacred, and, to a lesser extent, those that are considered sacred, the sacred spaces may need to be recreated at each gathering. Intensive interpretation adds meaning to a sacred space and reinforces its sacrality.

- There needs to be a variety of sacred spaces within Messy Church. Each of the seven monastic sacred spaces has a particular focus and function. Within Messy Church, it is important to ensure that there are different sacred spaces to facilitate different types of encounter with each other and with God. It is important to allow space for quiet reflection, sharing, impromptu conversation, corporate worship and nourishment, decision making and productivity. These different spaces should work together to create a sustainable church and a transformed community.

- Time should be allowed for silence and prayer. Working with today's 'I'm bored' generation, it is tempting to fill up all the available time, echoing the frenetic lives we lead. However, it is also important to create an opportunity for the participants at Messy Church to become comfortable with silence and reflective prayer as a way of encountering God. Alongside all the exciting activities that are planned, it is important to provide space for quieter, more reflective and prayerful activities.

- Different ecumenical traditions should be recognised. If a Messy Church is aligned to one particular denomination, it should honour ecumenical traditions within the format of the celebration. This principle extends to the use of liturgy, rituals and symbols that are familiar to the families who are attending Messy Church. However, these actions and objects should always point to something deeper, something beyond themselves. Regular ritualisation creates familiarity, which is an argument for ensuring that Messy Church happens more often (perhaps once a month) rather than less often.

- It is also important to acknowledge different learning styles and the need for holistic development. In children's work, it has long been recognised that people have different learning preferences. Not all are auditory learners (the most common form of instruction in the church). Some are visual learners, while others prefer to learn kinaesthetically, through movement or tactile experiences. The activities that are planned therefore need to accommodate a range of learning stimuli, to aid holistic early childhood development. The skills to develop include:
  - fine motor skills (hand–eye coordination)
  - gross motor skills (use of the big muscles in the body)
  - language skills (through conversation)
  - cognitive development (awareness of cause and effect, and logic)
  - social/emotional skills (through being with other people)
  - self-help (learning to be independent).

- It is important that sacred space is a place of safety and trust. Places that are accessible to the public must satisfy the legal requirements for health and safety, both from a physical perspective and in terms of ensuring that those involved in leading and helping do not pose any danger to children and families.[26] If sacred spaces are to represent and facilitate encounter with God, they should be welcoming, accessible and non-judgemental. It is in this safe environment that people will be able to be honest with themselves, each other and God.

- If possible, make use of the wild or natural environment. Just as religion and art are inextricably linked, and creative activities reflect the creative nature of God, so there is a strong relationship between the natural environment and sacred space. The beauty of the 'wild outdoors' has often provided a way for people to encounter the sacred. Our ancient ancestors intuitively used nature as a sacred space, together with rituals that resonated with natural forces. The myriad works of music, art and literature that acknowledge the splendour and grandeur of the natural environment are testament to its importance.

Conclusion

Families attending Messy Church are not necessarily familiar with the sacred space of the chapel—the structure where regular Sunday worship occurs. By creating a tailored and customised sacred space for the community, Messy Church provides a unique opportunity to show that church is far more than chapel (the place of liturgy, ritual and sacrament).

Messy Church has a responsibility to the families who are seeking an encounter with God, to provide the most conducive environment for it. Often, this can be done without the exorbitant spending associated with new buildings, by paying attention to the more immediate spaces that are created and used. Creating sacred space has far more to do with a consciousness of community and an attitude towards inclusivity than the architecture of the building. The creation of space that encourages an awareness of the sacred can transform the lives of individuals, families and communities as it facilitates worship of and encounter with God.

MESSY CHURCH AND THE SACRAMENTS

Philip North is the Bishop of Burnley in the Diocese of Blackburn. Born in London, he has served in parishes in Sunderland and Hartlepool and spent six years as Priest Administrator of the Shrine of Our Lady of Walsingham. After that, he became Team Rector of the parish of Old St Pancras in Camden Town, where his team formed a Messy Church that regularly celebrated the Eucharist.

What is 'church'?

In her book *Natural Symbols*[1], anthropologist Mary Douglas analyses the conditions under which groups of people abandon their rituals. Ritual, she claims, is a form of communication that gives definition and identity to a culture, and when that culture is under pressure or in decline, it first seeks to explain its rituals in rational terms and then gives them up altogether. One of many examples she draws on is the Roman Catholic practice of abstaining from meat on a Friday. At first, that ritual is unquestioningly followed and becomes a means of defining the community. But as the identity of the community comes under pressure, the ritual is first explained ('we abstain from meat on Friday in order to save money that can be given to the poor') and then abandoned.

A feature of human organisations and communities that are under pressure or in decline is that they become embarrassed by their rituals, language and traditions. They seek first to rationalise or reinterpret them and then they drop them as no longer convenient. This may be an explanation for our confusion over the meaning of the word 'church', a debate that lies behind a great deal of the controversy that Messy Church can arouse. In many parts of contemporary Anglicanism, we are losing hold of any sense of the church as something that has a supernatural or transcendent dimension. Rather, we rationalise it and understand it as a purely human phenomenon, a voluntary gathering of like-minded Christians, an earthbound organisation that is contingent, awaiting the coming of the kingdom, when it will no longer need to exist. At times, indeed, the word 'church' is seen as actively unhelpful, indicating a dry, dusty, irrelevant institution that needs to be reimagined, reinvented or renamed. Many fresh expressions will go to great lengths to avoid even calling themselves 'church'.

Unsurprisingly, then, we end up with confusion about what 'church' or 'the church' actually is. We are entering a realm in which any group of people with any sort of vaguely Christian intention can be named 'church'. Schoolchildren attending assembly are surprised to be told they are 'church'. Mums attending a parents and tots group find themselves on the Church of England's attendance statistics because a prayer has been said there. If people aren't going to church, just rename the groups they are attending as 'church' and the problem is solved. Humpty Dumpty lives![2]

The answer, as always, is to return to the Bible, which is incredibly rich in language and imagery to describe the church. The church is the bride (Matthew 9:15), covenanted in an everlasting marriage with the Son. It is the new Israel (Galatians 6:16), God's people chosen for all eternity. It is the new temple (Ephesians 2:21), the place where Godhead and humanity meet. It is the holy people of God (Colossians 1:12). What is interesting about much of this imagery is that it makes no clear distinction between the church on earth and the church in heaven. To be part of the church here and now is to be part of the same church for all eternity. There is only one church, one body of Christ, which exists in a way that is, at one and the same time, contemporary and eschatological, earthly and heavenly, here and still to come. Christ is equally incarnate both in heaven as the ascended Lord and here on earth in his body. The church therefore both announces salvation and constitutes salvation, for to be part of it is to take one's place within the company of Christ's redeemed people.

There is a tendency in some Anglican quarters to be embarrassed by so robust an ecclesiology. So Graham Tomlin, in his fascinating book *The Widening Circle*, writes, 'Now the church is not the incarnate Son… Too close an identification of the church with Christ brings danger. The church is fallen in a way that Christ is not.'[3] This definition of the church lacks the eschatological dimension that we find so richly in scripture. Of course, in its life on earth, the church is made up of sinners who get things wrong and make mistakes. That is entirely consistent with the fact that God is a God who chooses the weak. But this earthly church is nonetheless an expression of the true and eternal Church of which we are fully a part and which, in its fullness, is faultless as Christ is faultless.

Such a strong understanding of the church raises an important question. If the church is one with Christ, how is it constituted? Its heavenly existence may be clear, but how can we know where and how it is located here on earth? Again we turn to the scriptures, to two of the great commandments that Christ gives his church: 'Go therefore and make disciples of all nations, baptising them in the name of the Father and of the Son and of the Holy Spirit' (Matthew 28:19, NRSV) and 'Do this in remembrance of me' (1 Corinthians 11:24, NRSV). From the very first days, the church has admitted new members through baptism, for through washing in water we die with Christ in order to rise with him and so become part of the new creation. Again, from its very inception the church has expressed communion with Christ through the Eucharist, for through the ritual breaking of bread and drinking from the common cup, Christ has promised to be with his church until he returns in glory. In its inmost essence, the church on earth is sacramental. It is not the church that makes the sacraments. It is the sacraments that make the church.[4]

Some might argue that I am downplaying the role of the Bible in the life of the church, that we are a people of the word as much as a people of the sacraments. But this dichotomy is an entirely false one. To be a people of the book *is* to be a people of the sacraments. One points to the other. It was only when they broke bread that the disciples on the road to Emmaus realised that their hearts had burnt within them as Christ had taught them from the scriptures.

We are 'church' because we share in Christ and in each other through the sacraments. We cannot decide that any particular group of people is 'church' just because we call them 'church', any more than we can decide that a dog is a cat just because we call it a cat. Whatever we call it, a dog is a dog because it has the DNA of a dog, and, in the same way, the church is the church because it has the DNA of the sacraments. If Messy Church is to be fully church, it has to find ways of becoming sacramental.

The sacraments and evangelism

Already, though, I hear a practical objection forming on many lips: 'That sounds fine, but the trouble is, it doesn't work.' In an evangelistic context and in an unchurched culture, it seems to be a generally accepted fact that the sacraments are a barrier to evangelism. People argue that they are too staid and formulaic, that they have too many rules and restrictions, that they are complicated and hard to understand, that contemporary people just don't 'get' them. Therefore, many churches who wish to develop the ministry of evangelism downplay or even abandon the sacraments. This is especially so in Messy Church, where many would suggest that the (supposedly) inherent formality of sacramental worship is entirely at odds with the ethos of the gathering.

There are two responses to this argument, the first theological (why we celebrate the sacraments) and the second practical (how we celebrate the sacraments). But before launching into either, let me tell a story. Stuart was 14 years old when I met him. He had come to the youth pilgrimage at Walsingham not for any devotional reason but because he fancied one of the girls in the group, whom he knew from school, and he had managed to persuade the soft-touch vicar to give him a place. He was a tough kid who had no time for church. But then, during a late-night eucharistic devotion, Stuart came to find me. He was in floods of tears. 'Every time I look at that bread on that table, I just burst into tears, and I don't know why!' he said. I told him that he was crying because he had met with Jesus, the bread of life. He made his confession, went to find the soft-touch vicar and was later baptised and confirmed. A teenager was brought to faith through an encounter with Jesus in the sacraments.

Stuart became a Christian through staring at something physical, which in some way drew him out of himself and pointed him to Christ. A physical boy could relate to the physical—and that is why God gives us the gift of the sacraments. A sacrament is classically defined as an outward and visible sign of an inward and spiritual grace. Our gracious God relates to our physicality by using physical means to communicate to us his saving presence. Bread, wine, water, oil and touch become effective channels for divine grace to break into the world, bringing life and love and salvation. Through the sacraments, the redemptive power of the cross is made contemporary reality.

Once we accept this basic principle, the sacraments become not just an event but a lifestyle, not just one choice from the drop-down list of worship options but a blueprint for radical gospel lives. For example, in the Eucharist we see the dignity of the human person, for ordinary men and women are given the gift of bread and wine, which conveys the living, physical presence of Christ. So, to live eucharistically is to understand and acknowledge the dignity and preciousness of the human person, born or unborn. We cannot sincerely meet Jesus in the Eucharist without then seeking to meet him and serve him in the poor and the lonely, the victimised and the forgotten, the refugee and the stranger.

Again, in the Eucharist we see a vision of a flourishing human society, as rich and poor, male and female, black and white, powerful and powerless stand side by side to receive the same gift. So, to live eucharistically means to seek to build a world which reflects the heavenly kingdom that is thrown open to us in the Eucharist. That means challenging unjust structures, seeking reconciliation and right relationship, addressing the causes of poverty and ensuring that the young have the best possible start in life. It is no coincidence that the Anglo-Catholic movement has always thrived in areas of great poverty and need, because implicit within the sacramental life is a powerful vision of human flourishing and loving interrelationship.

There can be no more radical, prophetic or life-transforming act than to regenerate human life in the water of baptism or to renew human life in the breaking of bread, and this means that rather than asking why we celebrate the sacraments, we need to ask ourselves some very different questions. How dare we deny people this gift? On what authority do we claim that the sacraments are a barrier to evangelism when in those sacraments we gaze upon and share in the very life of Jesus? Who are we to decide that people are too ill-informed or too immature or too 'unspiritual' to understand them? Only when bread was broken did the disciples on the road to Emmaus see Jesus. And that is our task also— to bring people to Jesus in the sacraments.

The question therefore changes again: how can we reimagine and celebrate the Eucharist such that an all-age group and an unchurched generation can find Jesus within it? The issue moves from the theological to the practical. It becomes an issue of imagination and liturgical dexterity rather than of principle—and that is where we turn next.

Celebrating the sacraments in Messy Church

The impact of Messy Church in the life of the local church over the past 13 years has been remarkable. However, there seem to be emerging two very distinct ways in which this resource is being used at a strategic level, and it is very important that the leaders of local churches make a clear decision about which route they are taking.

For many churches, Messy Church is pre-evangelistic. It is seen as a way to make contact with families they would otherwise struggle to meet. The families may be drawn from schools, uniformed groups or baptisms, weddings and funerals, and the intention of Messy Church is to build relationships and grow the fringe of the church. However, Messy Church in this context is seen as part of a journey to more traditional membership of the church rather than representing the fullness of church life for its members.

In this context, the introduction of a sacramental dimension to Messy Church is not so essential, because the assumption is that people will grow into the sacramental life as and when they become part of a traditional congregation. However, at the same time, there may be reasons why such Messy Churches will choose to develop a sacramental side to their life. In Camden we had 'Messy Mass' at least once a term so that members could experience the Eucharist, become intrigued by it and develop some sense of what would await them if they moved on to Sunday Mass attendance (as, indeed, several of them did). We did not baptise because we did not envisage Messy Church to be people's primary unit of Christian belonging.

In many other contexts, however, Messy Church is seen as much more than a pre-evangelistic, all-age worship activity. It is a fresh expression; it is 'church' for those people attending. There is no intention of its becoming transitional or part of a journey to something fuller. In this setting, there is a greater challenge to the leadership of Messy Church because there is a profound need to engage at some level with the sacraments. How can church be church if its members are unbaptised? How can church be church if it never shares in the gift of the Eucharist? There is an incompleteness that must be addressed—or, to put it more positively, Jesus is offering these churches even greater riches.

Yes, but how?

Common objections to the use of the sacraments in Messy Church are the presumed formality and rigidity of liturgy, the incompatibility of 'traditional' worship with the informal feel of Messy Church, and the problem of receiving Holy Communion, which is often seen as a point of division or even exclusion. With sufficient imagination and conviction, though, the sacraments are not just compatible with Messy Church; they enhance it enormously. Leaders will need to give careful attention to the following areas.

- **Theme:** Just as in a usual celebration, a Messy Eucharist needs a clear theme, which is explored in the craft activities. In the Eucharist it is best to have just one reading and to think carefully about how it is presented.

- **Setting:** Eucharistic worship when significant numbers of children are present needs to be both accessible and engaging, but also to point participants beyond themselves to the transcendence of heaven. It is therefore important to move from the activities area to a different and well-prepared setting, and to create a sense of gathering for a meal around a table. The good use of lighting matters; dimming the lights during the Eucharistic Prayer can focus people's attention. Robes can be beneficial in demonstrating to participants that something 'different' is happening and are also an invaluable teaching aid.

- **Music:** Good liturgy is a partnership between the person presiding and the musician. The choice of songs is vital, and there are also many musical resources for the liturgy that can help people to engage—for example, sung responses to the Eucharistic Prayer.

- **Style of presidency:** There is a real challenge to the president, who needs to make liturgy accessible but not dumbed down to the point of banality. The priest needs to have a deep trust in what s/he is doing and resist the temptation to gloss over things, over-explain or apologise. One option is to have a second person who stands at the lectern and gives short and simple explanations about each movement of the liturgy, leaving the priest free to focus on presiding.

- **Liturgy:** The key change in understanding in this area is to approach liturgy in terms of shape rather than words. In the Eucharist we meet Jesus in three ways—in scripture, in each other and in Communion—and this is what gives shape to the celebration. Within that structure, it is important to use as few liturgical texts as possible. *Common Worship* actually enables far more flexibility than is often presumed, and so allows immense scope for imagination. The *Common Worship* prayers for use when children are present are brisk and easy to follow.[5] Minimal liturgical responses can be shown on a screen (and, indeed, are learnt surprisingly easily). Below is a draft liturgy that shows how all of this can be translated into practice. The main principle is to keep the liturgy moving along, though without unseemly rush. In this way the Eucharist can be celebrated quite happily within the timeframe of a normal Messy Church celebration. Optional sections in the draft liturgy are shown in italics.

Shape	Section	Liturgy	Notes
	Opening song		
Meeting Jesus in the word	Greeting	The Lord be with you. **And also with you.**	
	Penitential rite	*Sung, for example…*	*This is optional, and there is some argument for going straight from the greeting into the Gospel.*
	Gospel	Hear the Gospel of our Lord Jesus Christ according to… This is the Gospel of the Lord. **Praise to you, O Christ.**	There needs to be at least some direct quotation from the scripture, but otherwise the Gospel can be told as story, acted out or presented in an engaging way.
	Talk		Like any other Messy Church talk, but no more than seven minutes long.
	Intercessions	*Sung response, such as 'Lord, hear our prayer.'*	Intercessions will usually have been prepared during the craft activities and can be as imaginative as you like.

Shape	Section	Liturgy	Notes
Meeting Jesus in each other	Peace	The peace of the Lord be always with you. **And also with you.**	This can be shared in a variety of ways—a handshake or a high-five, or simply by joining hands as the words of the Peace are spoken.
	Offertory song		
Meeting Jesus in Communion	Eucharistic rite	One of the *Common Worship* prayers for use when children are present	There are many ways of engaging all ages in the action, such as a sung refrain through the prayer and use of lighting to create atmosphere. Gathering younger members around the altar can also engage them. It is important to create a sense of mystery.
	Communion rite	The Lord's Prayer; words of invitation	
	Communion	Songs should be sung or music played.	
	Dismissal and closing song	Go in peace to love and serve the Lord. **In the name of Christ. Amen**	

- **Holy Communion:** There should be nothing more natural than inviting people to share a meal with us, and yet the fact that some share in Communion while others do not is a common reason for not using the Eucharist evangelistically. There are a number of ways round this.
  - Think carefully through the words that follow the liturgical invitation to Communion, so that they are as inclusive as possible—for example, 'All are welcome to receive Communion, but if you don't normally receive, you may like to come forward for a blessing instead.'
  - Don't be too worried if it goes wrong; generosity and hospitality are more important than pharisaical sticking to the rules.
  - Consider admitting children to Communion before confirmation. Some churches do this for children from the age of seven, others from baptism.
  - Resist the temptation to give sweets or raisins instead of bread, which is merely patronising.

Baptism and confirmation

It is only necessary to use baptism within Messy Church if the second strategic approach outlined above is being followed—that is, if Messy Church is people's primary church.

In practical terms, it is fairly easy to include a baptism within the celebration. *Common Worship* makes provision for a rite of baptism in accessible language,[6] incorporating, for example, a shorter prayer over the water. This rite can be used in Messy Church with very little need for adaptation. Boldness in the use of symbolism can hugely enhance a baptism in the context of Messy Church, and this is something that the texts in accessible language encourage. Large amounts of water to be poured, an invitation to parents and godparents to turn around during the promises, oil for anointing, a white garment and a candle all engage the senses and so are both compelling and didactic for an all-age audience. Full-immersion baptism should also be considered. Be bold!

There are examples of confirmation being used in Messy Church, and there is no reason why this should not be so. Just make sure the bishop is well briefed!

Conclusion

It could be argued that Messy Church is implicitly sacramental. People come together, explore the scriptures and share in a meal. Those who try it find that adding a eucharistic celebration from time to time is a natural development of what they are already doing. All it takes is plenty of imagination and a bit of liturgical creativity. The Holy Spirit will do the rest.

If this chapter has done nothing else, I hope that it has described something of the joy and wonder of the Eucharist. In the Eucharist, ordinary mortal men, women and children feed on the very bread of heaven, share in the risen life of Jesus and anticipate the heavenly banquet that Christ, through his death, has prepared for all who follow him. It is because this gift is so unutterably precious and so compellingly beautiful that we must find ways of sharing it with others. To share in the Eucharist is to meet Jesus, and that surely is the only goal of evangelism.

MESSY IMPLICATIONS

MESSY CHURCH IN A POSTMODERN WORLD

Dr Sabrina Müller is an ordained minister in the Reformed State Church of Switzerland. She has spent the last six years researching the ecclesiology of fresh expressions of church for her doctoral thesis,[1] using participant observation and qualitative expert interviews. Sabrina trains ministers and students at the Centre for Church Development at the University of Zurich. She is a postdoctoral researcher exploring spiritual experience and discipleship as a paradigm for Practical Theology, and she is involved in further research on missional movements worldwide.

I have been to the UK 24 times in the last six years to visit and observe fresh expressions of church. It is obvious that these contextual expressions of church have the potential to interact in diverse, innovative and flexible ways with social change. In small steps, and often unseen, they engage and build relationships with postmodern people of little or no ecclesial background. In 2004, twelve different types of fresh expressions of church were discussed in *Mission-shaped Church*.[2] In 2012, the report *Fresh Expressions in the Mission of the Church*[3] described 14 different forms. In autumn 2015, the Church Army's Research Unit counted 21 types. This shows that pluralism in society is still reproducing an ecclesial diversity in styles and forms.

Because of this, I would argue that fresh expressions of church are one possible ecclesial answer that a state church can give to a pluralistic society: church itself is becoming diverse. Messy Church, as a local contextual church and a worldwide movement at the same time, appeals to thousands and thousands of people who might not otherwise attend 'traditional church'. Why? What are the cultural differences? Is it because people are expected to have less prior knowledge of the faith? Does Messy Church function better within certain cultures? And how important are the formation of relationships, the possibility of participation and the aspect of fun? As already shown in previous books, Messy Church is not 'church lite'; it is grounded in Christian tradition and centred on God, and it aims to be church.[4] And still it is a place where (certain) postmodern, unchurched and dechurched people want to be, to learn, celebrate and experience Christian spirituality.[5]

To explain why this is, postmodern thinking and the Sinus-Milieus theory[6] are helpful tools. So I will first give a short overview of the mindset of postmodern people. Understanding postmodernity helps us to recognise what people require, to acknowledge their spiritual needs. Both the postmodern mindset and the approach of Sinus-Milieus correlate with what Messy Church aims to do. The first part of this chapter picks up just a few theories about the nature of postmodern people. The second part tries to describe, very briefly, the Sinus-Milieus theory. With the help of these theories it becomes clear why Messy Church is so attractive for certain postmodern people, worldwide.

Postmodernism and pluralism

The words 'pluralism' and 'postmodernism' go hand in hand within the Fresh Expressions movement. Both are used to describe the change whereby both individuals and the wider society recognise and accept a multitude of opinions, religions, cultures, lifestyles and customs. A pluralistic worldview recognises and accepts political and religious beliefs that have heterogeneous origins. The UK, like the rest of Western culture, has made the transition from a monistic view of culture, religion, state, science, education and lifestyle to a pluralistic view.[7]

Because a pluralistic society has a huge impact on church, the *Mission-shaped Church* report looked closely at social change.[8] This term is used in the report for the shift in mindset and lifestyle from the modern to the postmodern, with reference to the sociologist Zygmunt Baumann, who has been an analyst of social change and postmodernity for many years. *Mission-shaped Church* recognised the startling and controversial aspects of the term 'postmodernity', but decided that it was best to use the term to describe social changes.[9] In the data gathered for my thesis,[10] experts in fresh expressions of church pretty much agreed on the changes they see in society. Bishop Graham Cray describes them dramatically: 'Because of these radical changes in society, where we find post-modernity, post-christendom, post-colonial, and so on, we are in a new world.'[11]

In the fresh expressions movement, consumerism, loss of religious education and knowledge, the fast pace of life, changes in family settings (such as a high divorce rate, a high workload and the loss of attachment figures), individualism, pluralism and the loss of community are described as the central changes. Bishop Steven Croft points out relational impoverishment as especially important: 'We are at a particular moment in British society where people are relationally impoverished, relationally poor. And they don't find it easy to meet people and make new relationships.'[12]

The church in general is often utterly ignored by media and society in the UK and in continental Europe.[13] By contrast, postmodern human beings show a rising interest in spirituality; they show an openness to experience; they like to participate, create and explore. They long for community and want to make meaning in and of their life. A change in the way relationships are built and communities function is also evident. Communities come together by choice and relationships are established because of shared lifestyles and opinions. As a result, relationships work mainly in networks, sometimes locally in very specific contexts. Furthermore, community itself is no longer naturally established through family, village and neighbourhood structures. Society structures now take multiple forms.

The Sinus-Milieus theory tries to give an order to this variety of mindsets.

Sinus-Milieus

Sinus-Milieus[14] began its life as a tool to study society, and is used by political parties, finance services, marketing agencies, television companies and others. The Catholic Church in Germany was the first church in continental Europe to use Sinus-Milieus as a tool to analyse and describe their work nationwide, geared towards a target audience. This was in 2005, when the Catholic Church in Germany ordered a study about religious and ecclesial orientation.[15] Since then, Sinus-Milieus has been used regularly in different churches.[16] Churches have discovered the importance of knowing their socio-demographical situation with precision, in order to gain an insight into people's lifestyle, worldview and behaviour, and to be in touch with them.[17]

Sinus-Milieus sort and order people according to their behaviour and self-understanding. Important areas of everyday life, including work, family, money, education, hobbies, free time, consumer behaviour and use of media, are studied closely and analysed. The goal is to describe changes in status, thinking and behaviour according to value changes.[18] The research produces a typology of groups of people (the Sinus-Milieu, perhaps best translated as 'social environment curve'), according to their priorities of values, lifestyle, aspirations, life strategies, fears and expectations for the future. Sinus-Milieus offer descriptions of segments of existing cultures in a common society. Because priorities of values, social situations, heritage and lifestyles are taken into account, Sinus-Milieu categories are not as fast-changing as, for example, lifestyle typologies.[19]

The international typology that is used is shown in the following diagram:

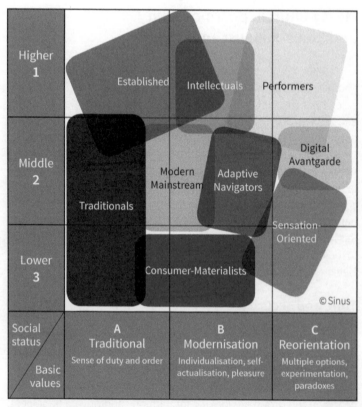

Sinus-Milieus diagram

Source: www.sinus-institut.de/veroeffentlichungen/downloads/Abbildung (01/06/2016).

The categories used in Sinus-Milieus belong to an international classification system. The vertical axis marks the social status (social situation measured by education and income). The horizontal axis marks the values system (basic values). Both axes have three sections. 'Sinus A2', for example, identifies people with a traditional orientation and a medium social income and status. It is important to know that there is always an overlap between the milieus; there is no absolute delineation. Strikingly, many fresh expressions of church can be correlated with a specific milieu[20]—including Messy Church.

Messy Church, postmodernity and Sinus-Milieus: an analysis

Anyone who visits a Messy Church knows that it is a loud, colourful and messy place. Kids are running around; parents, volunteers and elderly people are talking, and lots of creative possibilities for adults and children are there to be discovered. People of *all ages* sit together around tables, eating, painting, experiencing Christian stories in creativity, doing crafts and discussing life. If a steeple or pew is a symbol for inherited church, and an icon for the Orthodox Church, a table is the object that best symbolises Messy Church. Messy Church is about people sharing life (and Christ) around a table. A happy and harmonious atmosphere is what people often experience there, and this is what the Modern Mainstream milieu is looking for. It is important to remember that Sinus-Milieus around the world vary, but the Modern Mainstream is found in most societies globally.

Time and security

If the relational and child-focused environment that Messy Church creates is compared with the needs and wants of the Modern Mainstream milieu of the Sinus-Milieu theory, they fit and correlate very well. This milieu is called Quiet Peaceful Britain in the UK analysis; the people in this group are looking for harmony and private happiness, strong relationships with family, relatives and friends, and comfort and pleasure. They are striving for social integration and material security, and they are often defensive towards changes in society.[21] The setting of Messy Church addresses these needs and creates an environment where spirituality can be discovered playfully. In contemporary life, there are not many opportunities for families actually to do things together, to have time for a meal and to experience and talk about the meaningful things in life. In a fast and hectic world full of work, appointments and to-do lists, these times of being together have a sacred feel to them.

This chapter is not the place to do further explorations on the sacredness of experiences in a Christian community (or other faith traditions), but it is an area that merits further investigation.

Messy Church not only offers time together as a family, but it also opens up a safe and sacred space by giving people a visible structure. Even tough people are surprised by the creative ideas, Christian experiences and messy possibilities that are found in Messy Church, all within an apparently ordered and safe setting. Messy Church is structured; it has a time frame to it. If you visit different Messy Churches, you will immediately notice that the time frame (and sometimes the meal) differs from one context to another. However, for the families involved in one local Messy Church, it offers a fairly fixed structure (creativity–celebration–meal). The milieu of the Modern Mainstream is in need of this safe, predictable structure. If that was not provided, those attending wouldn't feel comfortable to explore spirituality and build up the relational surroundings that work so well in Messy Church. A postmodern and pluralistic world offers fewer of those safe and secure places, values and behaviours. The need for a reliable environment is especially high for this milieu, and Messy Church provides it, making Messy Church very attractive for the Modern Mainstream to visit and participate in.

Relationship and community

Messy Church opens up the possibility of meeting people with children of a similar age, to build up friendships and to talk about the schools in the area and about the sorrows and joys they experience as a family. Messy Church enables families to belong to a wider 'clan' and be integrated into a bigger community. It can even be considered as a replacement for the clan structures, with grandparents and wider family, that were a given until the 19th and 20th centuries. In Messy Church, children have the opportunity to interact with proxy grandparents. This is often very much appreciated by the Modern Mainstream, because it means that the value of family can still be passed on, even if natural family members live far away.

Often, volunteers in Messy Church are also from the Modern Main-stream, although the older volunteers might be from the Traditionals milieu. The Traditionals milieu represents values such as security and orientation to the status quo, rather rigidly sticking to traditional values (such as sacrifice, duty and order). They are modest and honest and down-to-earth, refer to themselves as 'the little people' and are often health-conscious.[22] The volunteers from the Traditionals milieu help to provide security and family values.

Participation

Modern Mainstream people appreciate traditional values and a good domestic setting, including good housing, a garden, a car, good marks at school and perhaps ownership of a dog. They value respect, good behaviour, love for each other, a good upbringing and spirituality of some form. But these priorities do not necessarily include 'going to traditional church', since, alongside these values, the Modern Mainstream are still postmodern people. If there is no opportunity for participation, and if there is no option to correlate Christian content with the daily experience of life, then these people are not interested in church. There is not much time in the week after the demands of work, so, if the place doesn't fit for the whole family, they will use their time differently.

The participative nature of Messy Church, with its opportunities to explore an experience-based spirituality, opens the door to church in the life of a postmodern/Modern Mainstream person. The setting offers space to get involved in a relevant way. This would not be the case for a person from (for example) the Digital Avantgarde, since this group are looking for nonconformist, no-fixed-dogma, creative and individualistic environments, where self-realisation, freedom and independence are offered.[23]

Because Messy Church is experience-based, easily accessible and a place to have fun, it attracts people not only from the milieu of the Modern Mainstream but also from the Consumer-Materialists. This milieu is marked by materialistic and hedonistic values. People in this group are striving to keep up, but often remain socially disadvantaged and uprooted, sometimes even in a precarious position.[24] It seems more difficult for church to build relationships with them, because they are looking for even more possibilities of experience and fun. But the simplicity of communication in Messy Church makes it highly accessible for this milieu. Most Messy Churches will probably have a majority of Modern Mainstream people and a few Consumer-Materialists, unless they develop next to or within socially deprived areas.

Experience

As we have seen in the description of postmodernity earlier in this chapter, the lifestyle and mindset of many people are very much experience-based. Postmodern people construct faith, truth and identity out of experience; only what is experienced and lived through turns into a meaningful reality in life. People increasingly need to know that God is involved in the details of their lives. Messy Church is about giving people room to realise and experience that involvement. It offers an accessible spirituality which is very 'can do': 'you can experience God'. The represented milieus in Messy Church are drawn to an everyday description of spirituality; God is attractive when presented as friend, companion, listener and ever-present reality. In contrast, there is much resistance to images of God as king, leader and judge, because these presentations of God are seen as a temptation to shirk personal responsibility for justice on earth.

Messy Church creates a specific space for experiences—individually, as a family and as an extended Messy Church family. The individual religious experience turns, mainly through creativity, into a shared one. Furthermore, the experiences are often relational ones, and that is what postmodern people are missing. So, through individual experiences in a relational setting, church happens contextually. Shared religious values and a sense of belonging emerge. It is not just spirituality that has to be experienced, but also theology, church and Christian community.[25] It is then that church gains relevance in the life of a postmodern Modern

Mainstream person. In this way, Messy Church fits very well into the general goal of fresh expressions of church as described by Rowan Williams: 'Simply, I think, to provide a framework for people to discover faith and discipleship.'[26]

Contextuality

The contextual framework of Messy Church allows people to discover faith and, in the long term, discipleship. Within pluralism there is no one-size-fits-all model any more (if there was ever one). A diverse, pluralistic and postmodern world needs to work very locally and to be grounded in its immediate context. On the one hand, Messy Church offers exactly that: it works super-locally. On the other hand, Messy Church is nearly a global movement; it combines the super-local and the globalised, networked world at the same time. Because of this, it is possible to be part of a contextual 'little church' and still be part of something bigger. This mindset fits postmodern people and raises their motivation for involvement.

It is especially important for the volunteers to be part of something bigger than the local. It opens up 'kingdom thinking', which, at the same time, is very local. As Dave Male puts it, 'So I think it is very much saying: this isn't just a community that gathers for its own sake, but it gathers for the sake of the world.'[27]

In my research on the Fresh Expressions movement (and Messy Church as part of it), the underlying topic of the furtherance of the 'kingdom of God' emerged as important. That's why church ought to be contextual, in order to be able to share life with postmodern and, in the case of Messy Church, Modern Mainstream people.

Conclusion

A good relationship between church and postmodernity can be described as one of facilitation. The church facilitates relational space for community between God and the world. This event is described by Rowan Williams: 'Somehow the church as a priestly people bringing the need of the world to God, bringing the promise of God to the world, standing in the middle, that's important.'[28]

According to this mindset, church happens primarily through an encounter of people with each other and God.[29] Through that, a dialogical-relational ecclesiology emerges, in which church is not defined according to a practice, institution or building, but rather according to a dialogical-relational event between the Trinity, Christian community, society and the worldwide body of Christ. Church development becomes a contextual offer of dialogue between different sides, with its goal to contribute to the kingdom of God.[30]

Messy Churches around the world facilitate this interaction by creating the space for postmodern people to discover spirituality. This is its strength. In the process, theology happens in a very hands-on manner, and is thus brought into everyday life. Messy Church combines social and Christian values, practical community in the neighbourhood with being church, by which a church emerges that is suitable for Modern Mainstream and, partly, Consumer-Materialist milieus.

The set-up of Messy Church guarantees Christian and ecclesial experiences in a safe environment. As such, Messy Church has to pay attention to staying contextual in every new setting where it emerges. It would not have done justice to itself and its potential if it had been degraded to a programme. The temptation to generalise the whole Messy Church movement and present it as a 'model' is ever present. This is partly because the Modern Mainstream milieu is globally widespread. In the long run, though, Messy Church is successful because of its very contextual nature; postmodern people, including children, and their ways of relating to God are taken seriously. Such a respect for individual journeys of faith is essential.

Messy Church did not start with concepts but with people—people who just wanted to be and do church with their neighbours. This relational, experience-based approach is the key with segments of a pluralistic and postmodern society, and it is perhaps also the key to changes in the wider church. At the very least, Messy Church provides a helpful, innovative field of learning for many long-standing churches, just as, within the Church of England, the relational and experience-based approach of fresh expressions of church has influenced and still influences its ecclesiology and therefore, in the end, its relationship to a postmodern society.

MESSY CHURCH
AND SUNDAY CHURCH
IN CONVERSATION

With experience in rural multichurch ministry in Cheshire and Somerset, **Mark Rylands** has a passion for helping churches transform their communities. Working as Canon Missioner for the Church of England in Devon, he set up a group to grow Fresh Expressions in Devon (FrED). Mark now serves as Bishop of Shrewsbury in the Diocese of Lichfield.

> There is one of two things we can choose to be in today's church… either… a mourner or a midwife: a mourner who weeps for the past or a midwife who places their hand on that which is being born and helps it to reach for life.[1]

I am a fan of Messy Church! As Diocesan Missioner for the Church of England in Devon, it was possible, from as early as 2006, for me to see its huge potential to reach young people and families with the good news of Jesus Christ. Messy Church seemed especially adept at inviting to its gatherings both those who rarely attended church (the unchurched) and those who had not participated for many years (the dechurched).

When I was appointed Bishop of Shrewsbury in 2009, the Church of England in Shropshire faced enormous challenges in reaching new generations with the gospel. Many of our congregations had few people under the age of 60, and yet they engaged well with local schools and with young families on special occasions—Christmas, Mothering Sunday, Easter, Harvest and Remembrance Sunday. Making and growing disciples of Jesus Christ, therefore, was a priority for us in enabling the church to make a difference in the community and to help grow God's kingdom.

In 2010, a Messy Church Adviser post was created for the Shrewsbury Episcopal Area (SEA) of Lichfield Diocese, and Cerys Hughes was appointed. Cerys had brought her children to church for baptism and had became involved in Messy Church in Wrexham. 'The children and their baptism were the catalyst for my ministry,' admits Cerys. 'I grew up in a church where young people were not valued or nurtured and church was only for people who fit in… I suppose I wanted to challenge and change that, so that my children and other families had faith opportunities that I didn't.'

Cerys' revitalised faith and passionate concern, combined with her ability to encourage others to participate and communicate clearly and winsomely the values and principles of Messy Church, led to many more Messy Churches being started and established. By 2013, the number of Messy Churches in the SEA had grown from four to 25. This constituted an extra 800 people, mainly under the age of 60, participating in the life of the church. Having a Messy Church Adviser has proved to be a good investment of the church's resources.

Through an imagined conversation between Sunday church and Messy Church, this chapter will explore issues concerning what constitutes church, Christian discipleship and the church's vocation to reach new generations with the gospel.

'When will they come to join us at church on Sunday?'

I have frequently been asked, by longstanding Christians, why families coming to Messy Church do not seem to make the transition to attendance at the main service on Sunday, to 'proper church'. The thinking seems to be that Messy Church is not church in itself but simply a form of outreach which will lead people eventually to join Sunday church; by some, it is viewed as 'church-lite' in the rather scathing way that all-age services were in the 1990s. It is as if Messy Church congregations have stepped into the rubber dinghy but won't properly be on the voyage until they have boarded the Sunday church ship.

The question this raises is 'What makes "proper" church?' A rubber dinghy and an ocean liner are not the same—they are made for different purposes and contexts—but they do share essential attributes that make them both types of boat. Similarly, for churches, is it possible to see core things in common despite the wide variety of forms? Through history, the church has manifested diversity in its organisation, practice and worship. Let me play you a imaginary video.

Imagine we are time travellers—think of Doctor Who's TARDIS®. We have stepped into a time machine and pushed the right levers. It is AD100 and we stand in the back of a room in the third city of the Roman Empire, Antioch, a lovely cultural centre on the banks of the River Arontes. We watch 80 men and women share bread and wine and praise the name of Jesus. We have tasted their worship and now we leave…

Fifteen hundred miles north and west—we stand on a shingle beach, leaning against the winds of the Atlantic. It is AD600 and we go forward to a stone chapel to join the company of the monks of Iona…

Back in the time machine and we are gone again—2500 miles to the south-east. It is AD1000 and we stand in the blazing heat of the South Sinai desert, looking at the walls of the fortress monastery of St Catherine. We stoop under its battlements to join worship with the army of monks…

We leave and head north-west for 2000 miles. It is 1740 and we stand in the drenching rain of Kingswood Colliery, Bristol, listening to John Wesley preach on horseback before the miners go down the pit…

Off again, to a Thursday afternoon in 2014. We have travelled 150 miles north, to Bayston Hill's church and community centre in Shrewsbury. We join 100 people—children, mothers, carers, fathers and grandparents—for creative activities. We sing some songs, hear the story of Jesus and pray. We then sit down to enjoy supper together at Messy Church.

Through our time-travelling eyes, we have seen many forms of the body of Christ, and almost every one of those forms would have difficulty recognising itself in the others. History teaches us that diversity is normal. Messy Church might look different from more traditional expressions of church but it is still 'proper' church.

'You don't need a lot to be real church'

Andrew Walls, in his enlightening book *The Missionary Movement in Christian History*, uses a similar image of the time traveller passing through history and stopping at key moments of the Christian era—the early church of AD37, the Council of Nicea in 325, the Celtic church of 600 and the Victorian church of 1840. Despite the different forms of church seen on the journey, Walls identifies several essentials that have been maintained over the last 2000 years:[2]

- the significance of Jesus
- the use of the scriptures
- the special use of bread, wine and water
- a sense of connectedness to Christians of former eras

When launching the Fresh Expressions movement in the Church of England in 2004, former Archbishop of Canterbury Rowan Williams said, 'Church is what happens when people encounter the risen Jesus and commit themselves to sustaining and deepening that encounter in their encounter with each other.'[3]

Mission-shaped Church, the report behind Williams' vision for fresh expressions of church, arrived at some values that it thought lay behind the formation of all authentic expressions of church. They were not written in a vacuum but echo and sharpen the values of the five marks of mission,[4] values which themselves are based on an understanding of the nature of God. The missionary church is to reflect our missionary

God and, therefore, is focused on God the Trinity; being incarnational, transformational and relational; and making disciples.

Following the above wisdom, you do not need a lot of kit in your knapsack to start a church. There would appear to be just a few core elements necessary, and Messy Church seems to have the essentials. However, there might be one or two fair criticisms.

'We rarely have Communion during Messy Church worship'

Until recently, there has been a distinct lack of the use of sacraments ('special use of bread, wine and water') at Messy Church.[5] There seem to be several reasons:

- Time is pressured if you are running Messy Church after school. However, there are now several all-age-friendly eucharistic prayers. Lucy Moore has explored this issue in one of her books.[6]
- The Messy Church movement tends to be lay led, and ordained priests may not be available to preside at the Eucharist.
- It feels exclusive, since many people cannot receive, having not yet undergone suitable preparation or confirmation. There are, of course, ways to include everyone, such as inviting children around the table, the blessing of groups, and linking the occasion to preparation for receiving Communion before confirmation.

To celebrate Communion can seem too difficult and best avoided. The issue needs addressing so that there are more opportunities for Messy Church congregations to share the family meal and recall the death and resurrection of Jesus. This would be a very good thing.

'The candidates from Messy Church will be baptised and confirmed at the main service on Sunday'

As bishop, this is a sentence I have heard, and I myself have baptised and confirmed candidates on a Sunday rather than at their usual midweek Messy Church service. This might happen for a variety of good reasons—because the clergy person cannot be available at the time of Messy Church, or the bishop has been booked months ahead for a particular Sunday; because of an agreed church council policy that says, 'All baptisms will take place on the third Sunday of the month at the all-age parish Communion service'; or even to help with the practical needs of the families concerned. It may be much easier for godparents, family members and friends, living at a distance, to attend on a Sunday rather than a Thursday evening after school.

Sometimes, though, it is because baptism and confirmation in the monthly Messy Church gathering have not been given serious consideration. Inadvertently, this can lead to a lack of pastoral care for the Messy Church congregation, which also needs to be nurtured. By neither celebrating newfound faith nor being allowed to welcome the newly baptised or confirmed and their families into the church family at the normal midweek gathering, a Messy Church congregation is denied a key opportunity for public declaration of faith and witness. It also misses the chance for strengthening the sense of belonging among those who gather for the local Messy Church—the sense that we are learning and growing together, and that we celebrate important personal landmarks as well as lamenting together over personal tragedy.

Shropshire is not renowned for being at the forefront of innovation, but I conducted my first Messy confirmation with baptisms in 2013 and have done several since. Messy confirmations are not so rare now in the Church of England. When we are able to baptise and confirm at the usual time of Messy Church, with the Messy Church congregation, there is a wonderful opportunity to teach about what it means to be a disciple of Jesus and to affirm the pilgrimage of the whole Messy Church congregation. Pilgrimage is a key aspect of Christian discipleship, and discipleship is another subject that often arises in the conversation between Sunday church and Messy Church.

'How can a congregation that meets only once a month develop real disciples?'[7]

Most Messy Churches are held monthly, some less frequently. The main method of discipling in British churches is through small groups that gather, often midweek, for hospitality, worship, scripture exploration, discussion, prayer and fellowship (such as Pilgrim, Life Course, Alpha and locally produced home groups). A legitimate question, therefore, is 'How are Messy Church congregations able to continue growing as disciples in between formal gatherings for Messy Church?' To bridge this perceived gap, some innovative pastors are posting material on the internet and introducing interactive forums for disciples to use.[8]

To become more effective, however, some of the creative section of the monthly Messy Church needs to be given over to training participants in the use of resources such as Daily Prayer, 'Pray as you Go',[9] *lectio divina* or the Examen. Equipping disciples to go on learning about their faith in the periods between Messy Church meetings is crucial and currently appears to be deficient in many Messy Church congregations. It is difficult enough to prepare separate materials for adults and children—even more so, therefore, to create material that can nourish intergenerational discipleship. There is a market here for someone! Unless seekers and followers participating in Messy Church find a way of sustaining and nurturing their own faith outside organised gatherings, in whatever way, it will remain less obvious how they can continue to grow to maturity in Christ. This is a question that needs urgent attention.[10]

'Yes, but don't *you* have a problem with growing disciples, too?'

Messy Church can easily turn the question back on Sunday church: 'How are *you* tackling the issue of discipleship?' Indeed, there are many parish churches that do not organise small groups outside the season of Lent. Given that small groups have been proven to be a key factor in growing churches,[11] it is disturbing that only four out of every ten churches provide such a method of Christian discipleship. Discipleship is a challenge for the whole church, not just Messy Church.

Interestingly, Messy Church also questions the way mainstream church has been doing discipleship: 'Is a small group the only or best way to make and grow disciples?' In her research into how Messy Church was helping participants grow as disciples, Judy Paulsen found that those interviewed felt that their involvement in Messy Church had led directly to increased knowledge of scripture, talking about God more with their children, increased attendance at corporate worship, an increase in prayer and enjoying more Christian fellowship. Her findings were that discipleship was indeed happening: Messy Church people were growing their faith in ways outside organised small group learning.[12]

'Messy Church is helping intergenerational discipleship'

One participant in the Messy Church at Ottery St Mary in Devon, Katie Drew, enthuses in particular about 'the great pastoral support that arises from everyone sharing the meal together'. Because children and carers feel they are in a safe space, carers have time to talk with the other people around. Katie feels that her faith grew as a direct result of the discussion at mealtimes and the friendships she made and maintained there. It also gave her a way to revisit spiritual matters that had been raised at Messy Church with her children back at home—especially through the act of saying grace and engaging in conversation together at supper. It might be argued that the mealtime at Messy Church enables a better experience of hospitality than at Sunday church, where the only fellowship may be little more than the coffee time after a service. Messy Church, with its inclusion of all ages together in creative activity, worship and hospitality, seems to encourage the habit of intergenerational discipling. It opens up a way for growing disciples and establishing faithful families that mainstream church might miss.

'In some ways we are quite good at helping people contribute and exercise leadership'

Messy Church may also enable a manner of growing disciples that is close to Jesus' way, as seen in the Gospels.[13] Jesus' discipling technique was all about observing and imitating. He called the Twelve to be alongside him, to observe what he did and listen to his teaching. Then he commissioned them to go out into the villages ahead of him. He was training apprentices. An exploration of Luke's focus on Jesus' mentoring and nurturing of the disciples is insightful. From their call in chapter 6 to their being sent to preach the good news of the kingdom in chapter 9, to their training of the 72 others in chapter 10, Luke gives us a frank and honest insight into the disciples' failures and Jesus' extreme patience and persistence. Jesus was prepared to work with the mess of human lives. He saw beyond the problems to the potential of his disciples. Luke shows us how God, in Jesus, does not give up on his followers. He takes ordinary folk and does extraordinary things through them. Indeed, there does not seem to have been a long period from the disciples' initial training to being sent out to proclaim the kingdom and then to begin training others.

Likewise, Messy Church can naturally disciple those who attend because it is not difficult for people to contribute and lend a hand. A father who is dragged along to help out with the craft activity may get drawn into listening to the scripture story at worship and then engage in a meaningful conversation about faith at the mealtime.

Libby Underwood says that in 2010 she was 'pestered' by her five-year-old daughter, Poppy, to attend the after-school Messy Church on Mondays. Having not been involved with church for over eight years, Libby was soon helping out and finding opportunities to lead at Bratton Messy Church on the edge of Telford. She is now an active lay leader in her local church. These are not uncommon stories. Church leaders with an eye for developing people's faith will ask both young people and adults at Messy Church to start helping with the leadership tasks and take positions of responsibility as they mature. In this way, Messy

Church has the potential to be fertile ground for growing disciples and future leaders.

'How effective are you in reaching new generations with the good news of Jesus Christ?'

Again, this is a question that Messy Church asks Sunday church. There have been many significant sociological changes in the West during the last century. Most relevant is the decline in Sunday church attendance and influence in society.[14] Indeed, the freefall in church attendance is a wake-up call to destroy complacent thinking. Sunday attendance of 9.8% in 1979 had fallen to 5.8% in 2009. Peter Brierley declares, 'The tide is running out.'[15]

'A missionary God calls for a missionary church'

The *Mission-shaped Church* report challenged the Church of England to face up to its failure to engage comprehensively with today's society and gave it a theological base on which to do so. It outlined the church's task as cross-cultural mission. It recognised that traditional ways of being church were not finished but could no longer, on their own, reach the nation with the gospel. Fresh expressions of church were necessary to relate to different contexts. Its theology of church planting was based on the incarnational mission of God himself, and it was the first denominational document to argue that church reproduction is a part of church doctrine.[16] Finally, the report emphasised, in its title and throughout, how mission shapes the church, not vice versa. Thus, it is not that the church has a mission but that the mission of God has a church, and the church is the fruit of God's mission.

'Sunday church's returner policy is no longer effective'

Mission-shaped Church argued that reaching the unchurched would become more and more of a priority—that inherited ways of being church, and traditional evangelism to the church fringe, would only tend to help a reducing minority of people. The report spoke of a time bomb ticking away.[17] The table below shows the full extent of the bleak scenario:

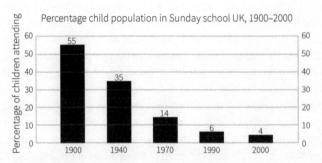

Source: *UK Christian Handbook, Religious Trends No. 2, 2000/2001*

Only a tiny proportion of children are now in the UK church on Sundays. The figure was down from 35% in 1940 to 14% in 1970, then to just 4% in 2000. This means that 97% of young people are not in church on Sundays.

Countering the gloom behind these statistics is research carried out by Margaret Withers, National Officer for Evangelism Amongst Children. Project REACH discovered that, in 2004, a considerably larger percentage of children were receiving Christian nurture, teaching and activity through midweek Christian clubs at schools and churches.[18] Nonetheless, her findings did not encourage complacency. There was a huge challenge here, and a need for fresh missionary thinking about outreach to children. The Church of England had relied for generations on a 'returners' strategy—that young people nurtured and brought up in the Christian faith would one day come back to church, perhaps when they were older and wiser, or when they had young families of their own. The report found this optimistic approach seriously flawed, for good reason; as the years went by, if things continued in the same vein, there would be fewer and fewer children with a Christian foundation to which they might later 'return'.

'Messy Church is reaching children with the gospel'

Messy Church, however, does seem to be reaching the missing generations. Children's church attendance on Sundays may have continued to decline since 2000, but there has been an increase in weekday attendance. All-week child attendance has stayed almost the same—around 220,000—for the last 15 years. This may be partly due to midweek clubs running in schools, but Messy Church is thought to be the main reason. The church growth consultant Bob Jackson describes Messy Church as being akin to a new Sunday school movement for our age, and sees the expansion of Messy Church as the biggest single factor in the growth of the numbers of children and families participating in the life of churches in recent years: 'By the autumn of 2012 the Diocese of Lichfield had 100 Messy Churches spread around its 600 parish churches. This accounted for around half of the extra children who were new to churchgoing in the diocese that year.'[19]

'Messy Church is not just for the children!'

Significantly, Messy Church is not only reaching children with the good news. It reaches adults too, particularly the unchurched and dechurched. Just as Alpha seems no more than a type of catechumenate with an imaginative and participatory way of helping people explore the truths of the gospel, so Messy Church seems to be no more than a creative form of all-age outreach.

Conclusion: recognising God's blessing

Like Alpha, however, Messy Church seems to be divinely blessed. As Alpha has helped thousands of adults to discover a relationship with Jesus Christ and embark as followers of him in their daily lives, so Messy Church is proving to be a way by which young people and families are being introduced to the person of Jesus and starting to belong to the local church. With 124 Messy Churches registered to date, it is estimated that some 7000 people now participate in the life of Lichfield

Diocese through Messy Church. Across the UK, there are more than 3500 registered Messy Churches. As average attendance is about 60 per Messy Church,[20] we can conservatively estimate that there are well over 200,000 people participating monthly in Messy Church—probably many more, as many Messy Churches are not registered.[21] Messy Church, like Alpha, seems to be a movement inspired by God.

I believe that our vocation as God's people today is to search for the next form of Christ's body. Rather than mourn the loss of old forms of church, it will be more fruitful if we play our part as midwives for the new forms that are emerging. In Messy Church, the time is right to help a new form of church 'reach for life', take its first steps, be nurtured and grow to full maturity in Christ.

MESSY CHURCH AND PLAY

Judyth Roberts is currently the Intergen Leadership Developer with the South Australia Synod of the Uniting Church in Australia, working to identify and train lay leaders of all ages. She was previously the Messy Church Ministries Consultant for the VCCE (Victorian Council of Christian Education) with a focus on advocacy and strategic training with churches.

At a local Messy Church, a small boy sits and watches attentively as his father shapes playdough into animal shapes, first a dog, then an elephant. Then the child reshapes the dog into something unrecognisable. They laugh together and begin again, their heads almost touching as they work on a new shared animal design. They are playing together, sharing a creative moment—with flowing ideas, a shared language, duelling imaginations and contrasting skill levels. They are making meaning and creating memories.

Play and the human need for playfulness have been attracting a lot of attention in recent years. Why is this? What is it about play that is important to us as humans?

Even the word 'play' has different meanings and connotations in our culture. We go to see a play, we play sport, we play games, we play up, we play around and children play. What could be a helpful definition of 'play' for the purposes of Messy Church?

What is play?

Over the last century there has been much research into play and there have been various theories about play. Maria Montessori noted that children's 'work' was to play and that they took it seriously. She discovered that self-directed play in an environment of choice offered the best chance for young children to learn through play. In his classic book *Homo Ludens*, Johan Huizinga described play as 'a free activity standing quite consciously outside ordinary life as being "not serious" but at the same absorbing the player intensely and utterly'.[1] He claimed that play defines us as human beings and that play *is* culture. In *Beyond Boredom and Anxiety*, Mihaly Csikszentmihalyi described how, when we are overwhelmed with chaos or unstimulated and bored, creativity is blocked.[2] He used the word 'flow' to describe the feeling of deep absorption which is also evident in play. In later work he propounded that two-thirds of creativity arises in the context of collaboration with other people.

More recently, Jonah Lehrer's *Imagine: How creativity works* reviewed the field of work on creativity and imagination, and discussed the importance of a balance of solitary and social aspects to creativity.[3] James Loder wrote about the pattern of the creative process in *The Transforming Moment*, where he described a fourfold way of knowing that leads to the transforming moment.[4] Howard Gardner explored play in *Frames of Mind: The theory of multiple intelligences*.[5] His work is widely known and has been influential in classrooms. He linked multiple intelligences to creativity and used case studies of Einstein, Picasso and Stravinsky, among others, to illustrate the value of creative insights through nurturing different intelligences.

Catherine Garvey, in *The Developing Child*, differed in her approach by rejecting the attempt to define play and, instead, proposing five characteristics of play.[6] Play is pleasurable, has no intrinsic goal, is spontaneous or voluntary and involves player engagement. She also stressed the social characteristic of play, and noted that play is linked with creativity, problem-solving, language development, socialisation and cognition. Her work resonates with Csikszentmihalyi's characteristics of flow.

While the focus of research was initially on children and their need for play, the strong links with creativity and well-being have led to a movement to encourage more playfulness at work, in our leisure, in our approach to problem-solving and in our relationships, and helped to form a desire to protect children's right to play as an essential part of childhood.

Play and Messy Church

Messy Church is inherently playful, the name itself creating curiosity and interest. For Messy Church, play could perhaps be defined as the underlying approach. Messy Church offers a way to redefine church for the majority of people who find many aspects of contemporary church boring or irrelevant. Messy Church is not trying to make church 'fun' (although it can be fun) but is reorientating church around relationships across all ages, hospitality, creativity and story. Messy Church brings a playful approach to planning and to the use of space and time, asking the question 'What if…?'

How might a playful approach be expressed and experienced at Messy Church? Playfulness is a state of mind which can be encouraged or suppressed. I would suggest that from the planning stage through to the cleaning up afterwards, a playful way of being together and working together could be a characteristic of Messy Church. Leaders can arrange meetings that are social gatherings of ideas and laughter, with people from many age groups represented. The way the space is arranged can provide opportunities for creative expression as well as social interaction for all ages. The way people are welcomed should be with smiles and an invitation to join the fun. Clean-up time can be an opportunity for further conversation and inclusion.

The key to a Messy Church that optimises the time together and highlights the Messy Church values is in planning an environment for play for all ages. Because the default expectation is that children and adults will be separated at Sunday church, Messy Church leaders need to be explicit and insistent on keeping all ages together. We need to be always encouraging adults to become engaged—not to stand behind children but to sit down next to them, both in worship and experiences, including the meal. Church leaders often feel comfortable about providing for children's play. We have a bucket of balls of various sizes; we can get out the balloons or cones and start a game. But what about a toddler? Or a grandmother with a walking-frame? Or self-conscious teens? Or over-competitive parents? At Messy Church, planning for play is a frame of mind, and this includes planning for a range of age groups and their relationships with each other. Play should not be competitive or rushed. It should be freely chosen, inclusive, not treated as a means to an end and not too controlled. In Messy Church we should trust that God's Spirit plays in the space too.

Play and experience

Rather than thinking about crafts or activities when planning, I try to consider what *experiences* we will offer at Messy Church, using an attractively playful space to invite people into them. I choose generative experiences that will bring people together to talk and explore their relationship with God. These range from cooking, using playdough or clay, painting, knitting and gardening to paper crafts. I also provide a reading space, a prayer space, artwork or photos on the walls to encourage contemplation, maps, jigsaws and woodwork.

This takes a considerable amount of time and thought, and often involves a number of volunteers who come and share their gifts and skills in their chosen creative pursuits. The unique opportunity at Messy Church is for whole families, sometimes three generations, to come together. This means that parents and grandparents and children can share their experiences and make lasting memories. Gabriel Moran, in *Interplay: A theory of religion and education*, has written of the 'interplay across generations' and its importance to Christian formation.[7] In his *Stages of Faith*, James Fowler describes the intergenerational faith community as providing 'an ecology of faith nurture'.[8] The regular interactions between people at various stages of life and faith develop-ment at a Messy Church are healthy and provide just such an ecology.

These are the kinds of questions that leaders might consider:

- How do I ensure that intergenerational conversations can take place?
- What if we ask a child to be a table leader?
- What if we ask an elderly person to share their faith journey?
- What might happen if we encourage older children or teens to play with toddlers and young children?
- How can we offer intergenerational service opportunities?
- What experiences in worship might bring people together?
- How can we arrange the tables to promote conversation?
- What is the best way to end our time together at Messy Church?

As leaders, we also need to consider the way we promote Messy Church, the way we plan for experiences and worship, and the way we plan meals and prayers. If it is too much like a kids' club, with everything aimed at the children, then parents won't feel welcome and will sit on the sidelines and talk among themselves. If we plan only with adults in mind, children will become disengaged and disruptive. Messy Church seems to exist on a spectrum, and the Messy Churches that are able to function within the middle part of the spectrum—holding the needs of adults and children in tension and encouraging the whole group to become more aware of each other—are the most effective.

Play, worship and prayer

'Love the Lord your God with all your heart and with all your soul and with all your strength' (Deuteronomy 6:5). How can we do this? We focus with our minds and quieten our senses to worship God. But if we worshipped God with our body and our imagination as well as our heart and mind and strength, it might look more like Messy Church. Children are experts at engaging with all their heart, soul and strength. Maybe many adults could learn from their interactions with children. Maybe many children and young people could learn more of the Christian journey and faith practices from older generations.

Erik Erikson, in *Childhood and Society*, notes the interaction across generations which he calls 'mutuality'.[9] He emphasises that people continue to grow and develop in important ways all through their lives, and that while children are clearly influenced by their parents, parents' and grandparents' development is also influenced in surprising ways by their children and grandchildren. Socialisation across the generations is vital to the growth and development of people of all ages. The generations need each other.

The Messy Church celebration can also be an exploration of aspects of play. Godly Play storytelling and wondering can be a fruitful approach. Jerome Berryman, in *The Spiritual Guidance of Children*, talks of 'playful orthodoxy', a way of giving children the Christian language system to help make existential meaning.[10] He argues that learning 'Christian' is like learning another language. The Christian language system consists of sacred stories, parables, liturgical action and contemplative silence. The act of gathering as a Messy community to worship God encourages collaboration, service, generosity and imagination. This worship can uncover gifts from the gathered group, especially when there is a direct connection with the creative work done beforehand. Ritual and play can be experienced as joyful, healing and nurturing in a worship space. The careful use of music and storytelling can create a quiet and meditative space or a louder celebratory one. Thoughtful worship planning can respond to the needs of those who share in the worship.

It is said that 'the family that prays together stays together' but it could also be said that 'the family that *plays* together stays together'. Playful prayer can be a way to open people up to new ways of coming close to God. Bubble prayers, flower prayers, finger prayers and prayer trees are just some ideas. Jane Leadbetter's book *Messy Prayer*[11] and websites such as Flame: Creative Children's Ministry[12] offer many creative prayer ideas. Messy Churches can act as role models, being prayerful and playful, showing a more peaceful, collaborative and satisfying way to be together.

At Messy Church, the conversations and laughter that emerge effort-lessly are God-given opportunities to share our faith as we share our faith practices. What does this look like? One Christmas, I was at a table with parents, grandparents and children, where we were all icing and decorating angel-shaped biscuits. The conversation was about when angels appeared in the Christmas story, and how many angels there were. We wondered about the appearance of angels, as the fact that they always say, 'Don't be afraid!' when they appear indicates that they might look scary. We talked about the fact that they are God's messengers and that anyone could see an angel, even today. We puzzled about how to imagine them, as they are not human: perhaps they could be classified as aliens, as they seem to come from another dimension. At this point, the children's angel decorations began to look decidedly less like fairies. Adults and children alike were fully engaged in both the theological conversation and the decoration. By the time we had finished, everyone had delicious angel biscuits to take home to remind them of the conversation and to provoke further wondering as the biscuits were eaten.

Enabling transition

Sometimes the transition between the different parts of Messy Church can be challenging. How can we move from a noisy, busy, creative space to a quieter worship space? How do we move from celebration to mealtime? How do we bless people as they leave? Clear routines can help. Some groups use a musical transition or a bell. I like to allow some time for transition, and, leading into worship, I offer a reflective space where there might be some artwork, candles, sand, water or pebbles. There are many rituals that can slow us down and help us get ready to enter a different space. Rituals that use natural materials seem to be inherently calming. The act of saying a grace before the meal and a blessing afterwards gives the mealtime a sense of being set apart. Incidentally, I strongly discourage the use of mobile phones at Messy Church, as the screens can be a distraction from the present moment with others and a barrier to intimacy.

Messy Church and meals

Gathering around a table and sharing food at Messy Church is a further way of being intentionally intergenerational. Jesus demonstrated the value of eating together by constantly sharing meals with his followers and marginalised members of society. The last meal Jesus shared with his disciples has become a sacred meal that Christians continue to celebrate as a sacrament. Few families today gather around a table and eat a home-cooked meal each night. Messy Churches are being counter-cultural in their generous hospitality and in role-modelling an alternative way. Sharing a meal is one of the most valuable bonding rituals. Rituals mean predictability and security for children; they give a sense of belonging and continuity.

At our Messy Church at the end of the year, children were asked, 'What did you like best about Messy Church this year?' The first child said, 'The barbecue we had in winter.' The next child said, 'The rocky road we made. It was yummy!' This theme continued as, one by one, each child mentioned a specific meal or food, or the fact that they enjoyed sitting down together and eating. I commented to one of the mothers later about their responses, and she laughed and said, 'You would think we were coming to a fancy restaurant, the way my children carry on when we come to Messy Church!' I wondered why, and she explained that at home they rarely sit down together for a meal. The way the table is set at Messy Church and the fact that the meal is home-cooked, with dessert as well, mean that this is always a special time for her young children.

As with everything at Messy Church, leaders will need to be intentional in planning meals that are delicious and not rushed, with people of all ages being encouraged to sit together, eat together and talk together. Leaders and helpers should also be encouraged to come out from the kitchen, sit down and share in the meal as a communal experience. Sometimes the best conversations happen over dessert and coffee.

Conclusion

Churches are among the few places where people of all ages and all ethnicities are welcome. The seeds that are sown at a Messy Church might be small but they are not inconsequential to the well-being of the families in the community in which your church is planted. The quiet work of weaving families and people of all ages together, to create a healthy intergenerational community that nurtures and protects children, often goes unnoticed, but it is vital work for the kingdom.

Jesus said, 'When you welcome even a child because of me, you welcome me. And when you welcome me, you welcome the one who sent me' (Mark 9:37, CEV). If churches took this verse seriously, surely they would all be exerting themselves to find ways to welcome children and their families. Messy Churches *are* seeking ways to welcome children, recognising that they can teach us how to live with the ambiguities of welcoming the noisy, the messy, the unpredictable and the outsiders. Are Jesus' words meant to turn us, smiling, towards children? In welcoming them, do we recognise ourselves as beloved children of God and come closer to each other and to God?

In most family homes, children and adults share the space. Most parents would assume that children have the same right to a space at the table, on the sofa, in the bathroom or in the garden as they do. Often, the space inside and outside becomes more playful when it is shaped to the imagination of growing children. The living room has a basket full of toys. Colourful cushions appear, together with ride-on toys and children's books. The television is often broadcasting children's programmes. The bathroom has a collection of bath toys. The garden is enhanced by a tree-house, a sandpit and perhaps a children's vegetable patch. But in most churches where there are families, children and adults get separated into specific zones, and rarely do those zones meet. When they do, it is a token effort. Sometimes a dark corner of the church is set apart for children. A token adult chair is put against the wall in a Sunday school room for a visiting parent.

What if we as a church assumed that children have the same right to space, style and content as adults do? What happens when we refuse to put people into separate groups? It becomes more playful! It becomes Messy Church!

THE PASTORAL IMPLICATIONS OF MESSY CHURCH

Revd Dr Irene Smale is Associate Lecturer in Practical Theology at the University of Chichester. She is also the Children and Families Work Adviser for the Diocese of Chichester and the curate at St Pancras parish church, which has run a successful Messy Church for the last five years.

A bishop once very kindly remarked to me, 'I am grateful for the way you do theology because you are out there working on the ground at grassroots level, and that's where the real needs lie.' Of course, working on the ground at grassroots level means that life will inevitably get messy, because people's lives are messy and they are very often messed up as a result of other people's messiness. I came to the Christian faith as a somewhat traumatised, disillusioned teenager whose life had been messed up by parents who went through a very messy divorce. Like most teenagers, I also had so-called friends who frequently messed me around.

Throughout my Christian life I have encountered situations where the church has messed up on more than one occasion because people just did not receive the proper pastoral care they so desperately needed. In fact, the church is very often perceived as being so out of touch with reality that it just wouldn't know how to cope with certain pastoral situations. So is it any wonder that people often disassociate themselves from the church and have a negative view of religion in general? Are we—that is, the church—any different from any other political or religious institution? I desperately hope, quite seriously in the name of God, that we are.

As we begin to contemplate the overwhelming challenges of the pastoral implications of running a Messy Church in today's postmodern, post-Christendom, chaotic, messy society, we must consider two key factors: first, the priority of safeguarding; and second, the human beings involved in our Messy Church. For obvious reasons, the safeguarding of children and vulnerable adults must take precedence over everything else in church life—but we must also safeguard, equip and train our teams who faithfully serve the families who attend Messy Church.[1]

There are four clearly identifiable categories of people who influence and are influenced by different aspects of Messy Church:

• the children who attend
• the parents or guardians who attend with them
• the teams who deliver the programme
• the parish priest or church leaders who are the overseers and pastors of the congregation and the services

Let us consider contextualising our Messy Church theology by exploring the cultural, social and economic status of the people involved in our Messy Church congregation and the pastoral implications of reaching out to our particular neighbourhood.

First, outside the church, the banner bearing the Messy Church logo is bright, attractive, fun, warm, inviting, contemporary and curious. It is also a symbol, an image and an emblem; an eye-catching, attention-seeking and appealing representation of the way you wish to introduce the message of the gospel of Jesus Christ to your neighbours. Who do you think is likely to spot the banner and be brave enough to cross the threshold of your Messy Church? How well do you know your neighbours and how well do they know you? Is your Messy Church located in an urban area, in a quiet country town or village, or on a residential estate? Are there local residents regularly passing by who might be tempted to wander in, but would not be sure what to expect? Is yours the type of church where people can simply walk in from the street and immediately feel welcome?

What type of building is your Messy Church held in? An ancient or modern church, perhaps. Or is it in a local church hall, school, scout hut or village hall where people are familiar with the layout of the rooms? Is the building clean? Does it look well kept from the outside and warm, clean, bright and fresh on the inside? Does it have adequate kitchen and toilet facilities and disabled access? Is the equipment you use in good condition and well maintained?

Most importantly, are you trustworthy? Do you have clear, visible sign-age, stating that you have a safeguarding policy in place and that risk assessments are conducted regularly? Are you known as a friendly local church where the congregation can be trusted and children are safe from harm?

By attending assiduously to all these details, you are sending out signals that you care. You care about standards of excellence; you care that things appear well planned and well organised; you care that people are going to enjoy Messy Church and have a wonderfully uplifting time. You care about health, hygiene and safety; you care about people's well-being; you care about being good ambassadors and you care about creating a church that is culturally and socially conditioned to meet the needs of the children and families you want to reach with the gospel.

Second, what type of people regularly attend your Messy Church? Are they the average nuclear family of two parents with 2.4 children, who live locally? Or are they people who travel a distance to make the effort to come? Are they single-parent families or extended families? Are they children who attend with only one parent, to give the other parent a break? Are they grandparents who bring the children to give the parents a break? Are they relatives of the team members, who only attend occasionally when they are visiting their family? Are they families from another church, who attend because their own church does not have the resources to provide a Messy Church? Are they people who are lonely, looking for something to do or somewhere to fit in? Are they families who would never cross the threshold of an ordinary church building but want some sort of wholesome, upright, godly, moral influence in their children's lives?

Third, who helps out on your team at Messy Church? How have they been recruited and vetted? Are they parents or grandparents of the children who attend? Are they retired people—perhaps teachers who have worked all their lives and are looking to volunteer their well-honed skills in their spare time? Are they people who have no other responsibility in the church but want to get involved in order to feel that they belong? Are they people with special additional needs who want to be included and to feel useful, so they offer help with laying out and clearing the meal and craft tables? Are they musicians who want to play in church but are not used in the regular Sunday worship services? Are they the backbone members of the church who are always first to volunteer their time, money and expertise?

If you are a parish priest or church leader, what about you? What kind of support and encouragement have you given your team, not just with Bible storytelling, praying, catering and crafting, but to equip them with listening and people skills in order to manage the pastoral issues that might arise in casual conversations over the craft or meal table? What kind of developmental training do you think they might need in the future so that they can flourish in their particular role? As Paul teaches, we all have a part to play in the body of Christ:

> So Christ himself gave the apostles, the prophets, the evangelists, the pastors and teachers, to equip his people for works of service, so that the body of Christ may be built up until we all reach unity in the faith and in the knowledge of the Son of God and become mature, attaining to the whole measure of the fullness of Christ.
> EPHESIANS 4:11–13

Now, before you start to panic and think, 'Hang on a minute, I didn't sign up for all of that,' I realise that all of the above questions might seem like an overwhelmingly daunting inventory of who, what, where, when and how. But these are, in effect, just a few of the immediate pastoral implications of running a Messy Church, before we even begin to touch on the individual pastoral issues that might arise *in situ*.

It is all very well getting people through the door—that's the easy bit—but what do you do with them when they begin to unpack the issues underlying the reasons that brought them along to a church in the first place? By posing the questions above, I am not intending to put obstacles in the way of starting up a Messy Church or trying to put people off getting involved. I strongly believe that Messy Church is one of the most successful missional and pastoral approaches to evangelism in this country today, and it is meeting an unquantifiable number of pastoral needs that are prevalent in today's messed-up society. To coin a phrase, Messy Church is reaching the parts that ordinary church simply cannot reach.

So fear not—help is at hand! When we begin to consider our pastoral practice, there is a plethora of helpful scholarly and practical sources to support the often complex infrastructure that underpins 'pastoral', 'practical' or 'ordinary' theology. For example, Bill Stone of CCPAS has drafted a comprehensive document, entitled 'A theology of safe-guarding', which identifies the three key elements of love, protection and justice in the doctrine of God that are paramount to this vital area of ministry.

> These themes of love, protection and justice combine in the Fatherhood of God, whereby he is our heavenly Father. This may be problematic for those who have experienced abuse by an earthly father figure, but it is how the Bible speaks, and Jesus encourages us to address God in this intimate way. The love, care, nurture and protection that God the Father gives his children is the true model of fatherhood, against the travesty of fatherhood represented by human fathers or authority figures who abuse, neglect or abandon those in their care.[2]

Love, care, nurture, protection and justice should be characteristic attributes, visible in the way we present Messy Church to those who dare to cross our threshold. The Church of England has published its safeguarding policy and guidelines on its website,[3] as do most dioceses, deaneries and churches across the Anglican Communion. Other denominations have similar and equally accessible guidelines. So make sure that your team members know where to find them, and ensure that they have attended a safeguarding training course.

Jim McManus also provides a very helpful set of slides on 'Some theological principles regarding safeguarding' for use as a resource in lectures, for self-directed learning and reflection, or for group work.[4] This or a similar training session could be a useful resource to help support your Messy Church team further in their theological as well as their practical understanding. It covers basic principles, including the following.

- Safeguarding is essential to the church's fulfilment of its calling and mission, given by Christ.
- Safeguarding is implicit in what Jesus intended when he said, 'Feed my lambs; feed my sheep.'
- Safeguarding is essential if we are to introduce people effectively to a relationship with God.
- Safeguarding is a sign of the kingdom—of justice, peace and integrity of creation.
- Safeguarding is an exercise of charity and of justice.
- Safeguarding helps the church to stay one, holy, catholic and apostolic.
- Safeguarding reflects the loving nature of God.
- Safeguarding is an essential context in which people can receive the sacraments and grow in discipleship.

Furthermore, for scriptural evidence underpinning the significance that Jesus placed on the care and protection of children, we turn to Matthew's Gospel:

'If anyone causes one of these little ones—those who believe in me—to stumble, it would be better for them to have a large millstone hung round their neck and to be drowned in the depths of the sea… See that you do not despise one of these little ones. For I tell you that their angels in heaven always see the face of my Father in heaven.'

MATTHEW 18:6, 10

This is not simply a practical pastoral strategy; it is part of the priority that Jesus gave to a theological understanding of childhood: in Matthew 18:3–5 he states, 'Truly I tell you, unless you change and become like little children, you will never enter the kingdom of heaven. Therefore, whoever takes the lowly position of this child is the greatest in the kingdom of heaven. And whoever welcomes one such child in my name welcomes me.'

In *Let's Do Theology*, Laurie Green talks about 'pastoral theology' as a type of transforming theology which becomes a productive and exciting tool for bringing together the crucial experiences of human living and the abiding truths of the Christian faith, because 'it puts faith back "in touch" with life'.[5] This is exactly the transformation process that Messy Church theology accomplishes. It puts faith back in touch with the lives of ordinary people. People who would never have dreamed of crossing the threshold of a church now find themselves once a month at Messy Church, discussing a simple Bible story that not only resonates with the craft they are enjoying making with their children but also gives insight into and lends meaning to their current situation in life. They have this one amazing window of opportunity to mull over snippets of Christian faith and wisdom, and to relate to them in ways that make sense of their lives. It offers a revelatory moment that provides answers to the questions they have been asking. Within that short window of a Messy Church service, they are introduced to the transforming power of Jesus Christ and find themselves as ordinary people suddenly 'doing' theology.

To take the theological importance a little deeper, in *Models of Contextual Theology* Stephen Bevans helpfully points to 'the translation method' most commonly employed in contextual theologies such as Messy Church.

Practitioners of the translation model... point out that it is possibly the oldest way to take the context of theologising seriously and that it is found within the Bible itself. Pope John Paul II writes that Paul's speeches at Lystra and Athens (Acts 14:15–17 and 17:22–31) are speeches which offer an example of the inculturation of the gospel.[6]

The translation model wraps up the meaning of the Christian faith in everyday language and thus clarifies the thinking of the hearers or recipients, so that they can relate faith to their everyday lives. This is what lies behind the thinking about fresh expressions of church introduced by the 2004 Church of England report *Mission-shaped Church.* The idea echoes the Declaration of Assent made by Church of England clergy: 'The Church of England... professes the faith uniquely revealed in the Holy Scriptures and set forth in the catholic creeds, which faith the church is called upon to proclaim afresh in each generation.'[7]

When we begin to consider the vital impromptu conversational opportunities that Messy Church opens up during a craft or over the meal, we begin to realise fully the pastoral responsibilities we carry. I recently had the privilege of baptising a five-year-old girl who had been dragging her mother to Messy Church for a year before her parents realised that perhaps she ought to be baptised. Neither of the parents were traditional churchgoers, but they very much appreciated coming to Messy Church with their daughter. I felt incredibly honoured to baptise her and welcome her into the church, as her family and friends looked on with a great deal of interest and pride. We followed up the family with some very open conversations about faith at the next Messy Church, and a year later they are still coming along regularly, because Messy Church is their church.

On another occasion, while I was helping out on a craft table, one parent quite casually said, 'By the way, I've been meaning to ask you: do you marry divorcées in this church?' You never quite know what you might be asked on the spot—but it is our pastoral duty before God to be prepared to respond in positive ways that reflect Jesus' mandate to love God and love our neighbour. So do not be surprised if you find yourself officiating at Messy Church baptisms or Messy Church weddings on behalf of your Messy Church congregation.

On a more practical note, I was recently made aware of a Messy Church that had identified two families who regularly attend but are living daily under such extreme financial pressure that they don't know where the next meal is coming from. So the leftover sandwiches, savouries, cakes and fruit from Messy Church are discreetly boxed up and handed over to them to take home after the service. This resonates, somehow, with that miraculous provision in the Gospel narrative where Jesus feeds 5000 people, and twelve basketsful are left over. If your Messy Church is anything like ours, it quite often feels as if we have just fed 5000, but miraculously there is still enough left over to meet the needs of people in desperate situations.

Social scientists have identified some common issues facing families today. The following list might include some of the pastoral problems we encounter when we open our Messy Church doors to the big, wide, messy world outside:

- families struggling with poverty
- unemployment and the dehumanising maze of benefit systems
- spiralling debt
- materialism and pressures from media to conform to consumerism
- accessing Foodbank vouchers
- single parenthood
- absent parents, who take on extra jobs to earn more money at the expense of spending less time with their children
- parents who place their professional life ahead of marriage and the family
- the changing concept of family
- marriage breakdown and divorce
- children who are raised in unions where the father of each child is different
- spouses who live far apart, due to the nature of their jobs

- the complex relationships of dysfunctional families
- parents who neglect the responsibility of educating their children
- adult and child illiteracy
- special educational needs
- health and medical issues
- behavioural problems
- addiction to drugs, alcohol, gambling, pornography, violence or internet games; lack of socialisation
- child abuse
- exploitation and trivialisation of sex, which distorts the minds of young people
- depression, anxiety and apathy

Some of the above issues might or might not reflect the experience of members of your Messy Church congregation, but each of us has a particular story, and each story is unique and incredibly deep. Sometimes people are reluctant to confide their circumstances to others, for fear of making themselves vulnerable, and they often feel embarrassed about their situation. I know of a single parent with two children, who, as a divorcée, was struggling financially. Although she was eligible for food vouchers, she felt so ashamed that she couldn't bring herself to visit the Foodbank. One of our team was able to go on her behalf, and she was grateful beyond measure. If we are not careful, we can easily miss what is going on in the recesses of people's lives—and that is why we need to be sensitive.

When my husband was first diagnosed with acute myeloid leukaemia, he was immediately rushed into an isolation ward. We were told he might die within days, even with treatment, because his case was so severe. I found myself, later that day, having to go to the nearest supermarket to purchase some items he needed in hospital. It was quite surreal, because while everyone in the store was acting normally, going about their everyday shopping, I was in a state of shock and turmoil. The checkout assistant casually asked me, 'Have you had a nice day?' and I honestly didn't know how to respond. I could hardly say, 'No—my husband was diagnosed with cancer today, and he could die this week,' so I mumbled something vague in an attempt not to lie, while fighting back the tears, and quickly headed for the exit. For days, I was in such a painful state that I could not talk about it; it was all too raw and unreal. So when someone unfamiliar walks into our Messy Church, we need to approach them with sensitivity, because we do not know what is going on underneath that brave exterior. It does not seem appropriate to share such personal issues in every context, so where can people go to get help?

Many turn to family and close friends—but what if you do not have any? As a hospital chaplain, I was called out on more than one occasion to help calm and reassure individuals and families in crisis. But not everyone who volunteers for Messy Church will feel equipped to speak into such contexts. Helpers are certainly not professional counsellors and should never be perceived as such. But most people are willing and able to lend a listening ear, which is often all that is needed. To be able to offload our worries on to a trustworthy friend can relieve a stressful situation and put things into perspective. All we have to do is listen and let people do the talking.

Acorn Christian Healing Foundation offers an excellent self-directed, basic course in listening skills that can be used in small group work with your team. It comes with teaching notes, a leader's guide and a teaching DVD.[8] For parish priests and other church leaders, something a little more in-depth can be found in Richard Osmer's seminal work *Practical Theology*,[9] which is a very useful tool. He identifies four tasks of practical theological interpretation that might help us to navigate the stormy seas of Messy Church pastoral care:

- the descriptive-empirical task: priestly listening
- the interpretive task: sagely wisdom
- the normative task: prophetic discernment
- the pragmatic task: servant leadership

Through careful priestly listening, the descriptive-empirical task gathers information, usually in an informal situation, that helps us discern patterns in particular episodes, situations or contexts in the lives of the people we encounter. So we should first ask the question, 'What is going on here?'

By applying sagely wisdom, the interpretive task draws upon social scientific theory to better understand and explain why these patterns are occurring. So the second question we should ask is 'Why is this going on?'

Through prophetic discernment, the normative task uses theological concepts to interpret particular episodes, situations or contexts, and constructs ethical norms to guide our responses and help us learn from good practice. So the third question we should ask is 'What ought to be going on here?'

Finally, by adopting a servant-leadership approach, the pragmatic task is to find strategies that will produce the outcomes we are looking for. So we enter into a theologically reflective conversation by asking ourselves, 'How might we respond?'

Conclusion

I hope that my brief observations from experience of the pastoral implications of running a Messy Church have been helpful. It is a tremendous privilege to serve the men, women and children who attend our Messy Church. It is not a task that we hold lightly, but it is both rewarding and extremely worthwhile. We never know whom we might reach with the good news of Jesus, and the little that we appear to do can often make a tremendous difference to the lives of the people who come to us, needy, damaged, hurting and confused in the very messy world we live in. Let's hope that in our Messy Church they find a safe, secure, peaceful, joyful and loving place, so that whatever the mess in which they find themselves, they can be healed and transformed by the love and grace of Jesus.

MESSY CHURCH AND EVANGELISM

Tim Sanderson is Associate Minister at Holy Trinity Church in Jesmond, Newcastle-upon-Tyne, and a Fresh Expressions Associate. He is part of the regional Fresh Expressions Strategy Team and has responsibility for a number of missional ventures, including a large and thriving Messy Church.

Some people might think this chapter is an unnecessary addition. After all, Messy Church has huge potential for effective evangelism among children and adults, and this potential is already being realised in many places around the world. One of the first things often noticed about Messy Church is its capacity to reach and engage with children, mums, dads, carers and grandparents who otherwise would have little or no link with church. From its inception, Messy Church was established with a clear commitment to be evangelistic. The underpinning principles state unmistakably that Messy Church aims to 'introduce people to Jesus through hospitality, friendship, stories and worship… to invite people into an experience of Christian community'.[1] Evangelism and Messy Church go hand in hand.

Numerous Messy Church practitioners have found themselves relating to people who are very new to Christian things and are perhaps taking the first steps in their journey towards knowing Christ. Other attenders might be those who are coming back to Christian faith after years away; for others still, Messy Church is their last attempt to stay in some form of church before exiting altogether. It is likely, therefore, that at any Messy Church there are all sorts of people muddling together, including many who might be termed 'unchurched'. The success of Messy Church in attracting and engaging non-Christians is hard to dispute.

So I was taken aback by the reaction from some fellow evangelists when I finally confessed that I was thinking of starting a Messy Church. They were incredulous. 'Why?' they said. 'Why would you want to do that? Messy Church is a craft club run by children's work volunteers. What's that got to do with evangelism?'

Why Messy Church?

Even if Messy Church was *only* a craft club run by children's work volunteers, that would still be a worthwhile and valuable venture, and it might have everything to do with evangelism. Despite the evidence, though, some Christians still appear to have a blind spot when it comes to the evangelistic potential that a Messy Church can offer, particularly regarding its ability to reach adults.

Why is this? Perhaps it is because they don't understand or value the missional impact that an all-age venture might have. Family ministry and all-age work can sometimes lack the credibility and appeal of youth work or more 'edgy' evangelistic projects, such as planting a church for bikers or surfers. Unfairly, family-based work can suffer from an image problem, its brilliance being obscured by unhelpful depictions of the work—endless craft activities, action songs, colouring sheets and children's workers who wear bright clothes and speak loudly and slowly! In addition, if Messy Church is understood to be predominantly a children's activity time with a few adults on the periphery, it is easy to see why some evangelists might struggle to take it seriously. Can the good news of Jesus be proclaimed effectively in an all-age setting with children significantly present, without an adult-focused evangelistic talk that outlines the full Christian message in clear steps? Unlike those with reservations, I believe it can.

I recently had the privilege of sharing part of my own Messy Church story with a gathering of pioneers involved in church planting. I watched their eyes glaze over when they realised I was going to talk on Messy Church. Before a word was spoken, I felt as if the room had already decided that Messy Church was not and could not be a serious evangelistic option for those wishing to engage with adults. It was only as I told stories of how men and women had opened up to the possibilities of God through this work that their attention was grabbed and attitudes changed.

I don't blame them. If our only experience of all-age ministry is a rather dismal, poorly attended church service with limp action songs and a patronising homily, it's no wonder there is little expectation or appreciation of what high-quality multigenerational gatherings can achieve and how they might relate to evangelism. Messy Church's appeal is first and foremost that it offers fun activities for the whole family. Its success, far from being limited by the all-age remit, is most likely due to it. It's important to note this point—and we will return to it later.

However blind some people might be to the evangelistic possibilities of Messy Church, due to its all-age ethos, there is a much more significant and fundamental problem for others: what is happening in Messy Churches challenges some traditional definitions and models of evangelism. Messy Church isn't evangelism in a familiar form, so some people struggle to be open to the possibilities it offers.

What is evangelism?

When the word 'evangelism' is mentioned, people often get mental pictures of putting up a tent, going from door to door, waving a Bible on a street corner and so on. Traditional evangelistic methodology is often modelled as the proclamation of a linear A-B-C message—'admit, believe, confess'—with the assumption that if someone is in possession of the gospel headlines, they will see the need to respond. Even in the more contemporary explorative approaches, such as Emmaus, Alpha, Start! and Christianity Explored, evangelism still takes place in an adult-orientated environment. Some of these methods may well be effective ways of reaching those who need to hear, but they can seem to be a long way from the average Messy Church experience. Those looking for a 25-minute evangelistic sermon with a rallying 'altar call' neatly shoe-horned between craft time and celebration will be sadly disappointed. Messy Church is modelling something very different from that.

There might be widespread agreement that at the heart of evangelism is the idea of restoring relationships between God and people. There might even be some consensus that evangelism, at its core, is about communicating the fact that through Jesus' life, death and resurrection, God offers the forgiveness of sins and the gift of new life, and begins the healing of the world. We might agree that, in inviting a response, we call people to trust Christ for the forgiveness of their sins, to become devoted followers of Christ, to be filled with his Spirit, and to join in God's community and God's mission in the world. Beyond that consensus, however, understandings of evangelism are many and varied. They vary in terms of their emphasis on concepts like proclamation or presence, point of decision or process, and the centrality of the individual evangelist or the transformative community.[2] To comprehend the full missional impact of Messy Church, we may need to rethink our tight formulaic definitions of evangelism.

If mission is understood as the entirety of God's activity to restore his kingdom to the whole of his creation,[3] then evangelism is the component of mission that desires or results in the rebuilding of relationship between people and God, as the good news of Jesus is both told and lived. 'Evangelism' describes the range of different routes by which people become followers of Jesus Christ as Lord. William J. Abraham captures this well in his definition of evangelism as 'a process of intentional activities having the goal of initiating people into the kingdom of God for the first time... (and seeing them grounded in that rule so that they can begin a new life as agents of reconciliation, compassion and peace)'.[4]

This is a helpful definition when considering the nature of evangelism at Messy Church, as it could be argued that the 'process of intentional activities' is demonstrated clearly through a number of interrelated components, all framed by generous welcome and hospitality.[5] Within Messy Church, these activities include story, play, all-age engagement, hospitality, worship, community and invitation. Much has been said elsewhere about hospitality,[6] but I would like to focus particularly on the role of story, play and all-age engagement in relation to evangelism.

Messy story and evangelism

Over 75% of the Bible comprises stories. When you add in the poetry and proverbs, you are left with probably less than 10% that is 'abstract' intellectual content. The power of story is that it helps people to interpret and make sense of what is happening to them and work out their responses. However, stories are also the ultimate in ambiguous communication, because, even if a story is enjoyed and appreciated, there is no guarantee that it will be understood as the storyteller hoped it would be.

In Messy Church, the story is pivotal to the whole programme, often forming a centrepiece to the gathered worship time. The strength of Messy Church is that the interpretation of and response to the story are far from ambiguous, as they are firmly shaped and informed by a plethora of reinforcement techniques. Through the themed crafts and activities, the wider components of the celebration time and the intentional conversations over the meal, much of the ambiguity of the storytelling process can be resolved and a shared sense of understanding can be developed.

Strongly themed programmes that retell and highlight the story and its application can enable a powerful and effective method of communication. So 'story' at Messy Church is much more than just a ten-minute slot. It is explored, reflected on, discussed and inhabited throughout the session, using a wide range of creative media. In one sense, the story is lived out together, and, by the end of a session, many participants have significantly grown in their understanding and appreciation of the narrative.

This is notable, since an essential part of the evangelistic process is the accumulation of knowledge of the Christian story so that its implications can be grasped. The Engels scale and other similar 'linear' models, which describe the stepped processes towards the point of conversion and beyond, concur on the importance of gaining a basic gospel education and understanding in order to consider the implications and reach the point of decision.[7]

Many who attend Messy Church begin with little or no knowledge of even the fundamentals of the Christian message, so inviting them to inhabit, explore and engage with the gospel narrative is essential to the evangelistic process. Talking about the human figure of Jesus will always provoke a response. Jesus is compelling, attractive and intriguing, and focusing on the Jesus story moves the listener from abstract and conceptual questions to a person. The questions about Jesus Christ are tangible and immediate and encourage response. In other words, when the Messy Church community listens to, engages with and retells aspects of the Jesus story, this is a way to introduce them to Jesus, his claims and his life-transforming possibilities.

So where the story in Messy Church is Jesus-focused, or explores some element of the good news of Jesus, this might well be a far more effective method of 'proclamation' than some conventional sermon-style evangelistic presentations. Perhaps, then, in their yearly programmes, individual Messy Churches might want to focus more intentionally on the life of Jesus, his miracles, parables and encounters with people, or on Old Testament stories that provide some of the 'building blocks' to the gospel message. The Christ story has the ability to stimulate all the senses and fire the imagination, and its impact on faith development should not be underestimated.

Messy play and evangelism

Fun, play and creativity are key elements for someone who is exploring and understanding their identity and place in the world. People can be open to new ideas, new concepts and new friendships when they are having fun. In terms of evangelism, this means that in the early stages of people's attendance at Messy Church, it can be more powerful to appeal to their imaginations than to their emotions or intellects. Play in an all-age context can be particularly significant for evangelism; through it, people may open up to the wider group and become more receptive to the context and values of the setting. In other words, people are relaxed and willing to engage.

Where Messy Church intends to engage with dads, attention must be given to the gender balance of the team and the content of the play activities. Without wishing to rely too heavily on gender stereotypes, Messy Church can be extremely effective at engaging with dads if some activities are construction-based, include problem-solving, offer very messy crafts or involve an element of competition or sport.[8] Conversely, where these are not in evidence, the proportion of men attending will be lower.

The strength of Messy Church here is that play is intentional and contextual. Fun activities such as crafts, games, construction and singing enable all generations to engage with one another—but also, in significant and deep ways, with the themes being explored. This is especially the case where the volunteers leading activities are well briefed and confident enough to articulate how the activity links to the wider theme.

Messy all-age community and evangelism

As noted earlier, part of the success of Messy Church in attracting non-Christians must be due to its all-age nature, in terms of both accessibility and content. Adults who would not usually respond to an invitation to Alpha or more traditional Sunday worship might well attend Messy Church, initially because their children enjoy the experience, but soon because they themselves are becoming more open. Messy Church aims to reach whole families and, while it is especially inclusive of children, it also caters for the needs of parents, grandparents and other family members. Where else might three generations of unchurched people hear the same story of God's love?

The very fact that Messy Church is an intentional all-age community means that the insights of children are as valued as those of adults. Children can lead the way in evangelism and are often the motivators behind parental attendance, the theologians who work out the applications of the Bible stories, and the evangelists who model an expectant faith and pursue the hard questions. It is unwise to underestimate the importance of children to the evangelistic process as they interact with each other and their families at Messy Church.

Messy Church aims to facilitate a positive experience of Christian community for all ages while dealing with the key issues of relationship building and trust. This is very significant in determining the evangelistic effectiveness of Messy Church. Through all-age relationships within a welcoming community, people are enabled to open up to the possibilities of God.

In *Making Disciples in Messy Church*, Paul Moore suggests that tools like the Engels scale are too linear and, on their own, might not fully describe people's journeys of faith within Messy Church. He suggests a more complex model—the Gray matrix. This combines the Engels scale with a second axis that describes a spectrum of feeling and attitude towards Christian faith and church, showing how open or closed someone is to the gospel.[9]

This more complex model is very helpful in determining what might actually be taking place within a Messy Church community. It seems that Messy Church is particularly effective in enabling people to travel along the second axis—the journey from being closed to becoming more open towards the possibilities that God offers.

Within my own Messy Church, I have witnessed this process of adults opening up in a number of ways—most strikingly through body language, as newcomers slowly relax and then begin to join in, and as they get used to being in the venue and spending time with Christians. There is an opening up towards each other and the team as relationships deepen over time, and this can lead to an opening up in their expectations of God, and perhaps to them reaching a place where they might ask the team to pray about specific situations. Likewise, people's understanding of God is deepened through the activities, conversation and storytelling, as knowledge is increased and more is revealed about Jesus. Here is an opening up to an experience of God, through the celebration times and involvement in Messy Church Communion and, for some in due course, in their serving, as they get more involved.

Most significantly, this opening up to the possibilities of God has been demonstrated in all ages and genders—boys and girls, mums and dads, and grandparents. Messy Church can be an effective way to help people progress, firstly, to greater openness and, secondly, in their understanding of and response to the gospel message. The emphasis on welcome, community, friendship and unpressured exploration seems to be an important factor in this progression.

Messy Church can also provide a safe space in which to explore faith as a family. Within the all-age context of Messy Church, the family has a shared experience that can spill out into the home for weeks after the event. Many Messy Churches produce take-home sheets or web resources to encourage this kind of interaction. Studies show that those attending Messy Church will talk about matters of faith in between events.[10]

One challenge to this all-age approach is the lack of success in recruiting adults on to Alpha and other discipleship courses. Reasons cited often include the difficulty of making regular evening commitments at this life stage, with small children, but more fundamentally attendance requires acceptance of a change of ethos. The move from an all-age to an adult-only environment can be challenging for parents who might be more comfortable in the Messy Church environment. A challenge here is for Messy Churches to think creatively about how to make spaces where families can continue to respond and grow in their faith—perhaps through Messy Church additional events or imaginative forms of all-age discipleship. Anglican Church Planting Initiative suggests, among other things, that all-age cells, parenting groups and storytelling workshops might be of help here.[11] There may be no single answer, but, as Messy Church continues to mature as a movement, it might need to find more cohesive mechanisms that facilitate transition from evangelism to nurture. Perhaps not everything can be achieved within an all-age context. Is there a need for adult spaces to address adult issues, and how might Messy Church create these opportunities?

Not-so-Messy evangelism

As we have seen, many of the elements of Messy Church are by no means new. The shared meal is suggestive of Alpha. The emphasis on storytelling and exploration resonates with Godly Play values. The themed craft activities could have been taken from a holiday club. The focus on hospitality reminds me of café church, and the high levels of inclusivity, participation and welcome are reminiscent of missional cells. But what Messy Church does is to bring these elements together and place around them a firm conceptual frame. Its intentional emphasis on being for those currently outside the church, together with its hospitality, invitation and strongly themed programmes, results in a context that can be effective for evangelistic purposes.

The gospel and its values are enacted through relationship, story, play and unpressured exploration. This is a holistic and implicit process that holds on firmly and intentionally to the goal of initiating people into the kingdom of God. The reality is that many missional ventures reflect elements of the Messy Church approach, or perhaps take one of them at a time. But in Messy Church, a single event has been created that enables the forming and deepening of relationships with non-Christians, includes evangelistic activities and offers a powerful invitation for non-Christians to join with Christians in all-age worship.

Instinctively and intuitively, Messy Church houses an effective combination of intentional activities that together build into a model of enormous evangelistic potential. Where Messy Church is at its best, where its programmes and values lead unchurched people of all ages to inhabit the Jesus story and, through it, to encounter the person of Jesus, we will see the evangelistic impact of this work coming to fruition. The full potential of Messy Church has yet to be unlocked; the movement is still in its infancy, and many Messy Church practitioners are only now beginning to see just how evangelistic these all-age discipling communities can be.

Paradoxically, for a movement that is concerned with values and exploration rather than fixed policies and stratagems, this is a formidably integrated evangelism strategy.

MESSY CHURCH AND THE CHALLENGE OF MAKING DISCIPLES

Stephen Kuhrt is Vicar of Christ Church, New Malden. He is the author of *Tom Wright for Everyone: Putting the theology of N.T. Wright into practice in the local church* (SPCK, 2011) and several Grove books in the 'Evangelism' series, including *Church Growth through the Full Welcome of Children: The 'Sssh free church'* (Grove, 2009).

Messy Church is just one of a number of inventive and pioneering approaches to Christian mission that have been developed within Britain over the last 20 years or so. During this period, there has been a decisive move towards local churches initiating all sorts of imaginative and exciting projects designed to connect with unchurched people and bring the love of God in Jesus Christ to their lives. Within the Church of England, these developments have been recognised and further encouraged through reports such as *Breaking New Ground* and *Mission-shaped Church*, produced in 1994 and 2004 respectively. Regular reference to 'fresh expressions of church', 'Mission Action Plans' and the 'pioneer streams' now in existence within theological training are all testimony to the way in which churches are seeking ways to proclaim Christ afresh to an increasingly post-Christendom culture.

Our culture might be post-Christendom but it is not post-spiritual. In fact, one of the crucial factors encouraging such fresh expressions of church over the last three decades has been the renewed thirst for spirituality that has emerged within our culture. Frequently vague, its nature was never more clearly stated than when, following the birth of their first son, David Beckham announced that he and Victoria definitely wanted to get Brooklyn christened but hadn't decided upon the religion yet. Suddenly (or so appearing, for Christians who have been slow to wake up to it), the search for spirituality is everywhere, even if the last place where many people are looking to find it is within a traditional church. Rather than accepting that the search has to exclude Christianity, however, many of the most dynamic examples of fresh expressions have sought to connect directly with this emerging spirituality and use it to lead those outside of the church further towards Jesus Christ.

Messy Church forms one of the most outstanding and energetic examples of this connection. Based on an atmosphere conveying welcome to all, Messy Church has used a potent combination of fun, craft, food and community to engage with children and their parents/carers, bringing the love of God further into their lives.

At least three symptoms of the changes within our culture that directly affect new parents (all linked to the upsurge in the search for spirituality) are being tapped into here. First, and perhaps most obviously, there is an increased need to find local community. With extended families living further apart (not to mention the increase in lone parenting), the network of support needed for rearing a child often needs to be sought elsewhere, leading many new (and potentially isolated) mothers in particular to take such support from wherever they can find it. Second, the need to find or reconnect with the values they wish their children to inherit is a powerful driver for many new parents, sometimes encouraged by fears (of varying legitimacy) regarding the growing cultural diversity within Britain today. Third, many new parents experience what can be described as a 'God moment' when a child arrives, frequently accompanied by the strong desire for 'something spiritual' to speak into the deeply moving experience that it has been for them.[1] In fact, with the majority of fathers now present at the birth of their children, this latter factor could be seen as dramatically increasing.

All of these factors, and probably many more, are being tapped into by the various Messy Churches that have sprung up around the country. The children and adults (not all of them parents) attracted to Messy

Church find a God who is prepared to encounter them through means very different from those more traditionally associated with church. The desire for creativity, fun, movement, interaction, food and noise are all strongly affirmed and used as media to convey the love of God and the message that he has come to rescue them in Jesus Christ.

How can this undoubted engagement be built upon, encouraging those encountered through Messy Church towards becoming lifelong disciples (or learners) of Jesus Christ? The great strength of Messy Church, like many fresh expressions of church, lies in the way that, like Jesus, it 'meets people where they are' with the love of God. But Jesus went further than this. He did indeed meet people where they were, but he did not leave them there. He called them to follow him, to become part of God's kingdom (or sovereign rule) and to have every part of their lives challenged and transformed. So how can the brilliant work of Messy Church and missional projects similar to it bring about such committed and life-changing discipleship?

Before an answer is attempted to this question, some words of caution are needed. Sometimes, impatience for answers is not a good sign. When people in churches that have started projects such as Messy Church (usually people who are outside the team implementing them) express the desire to see more 'progress' within the lives of those attending, what they frequently mean is, 'When will these new people start becoming more like us?' Many traditional churches are in decline, and one of the counter signs to this, to which congregations most aspire, is that they are managing to attract new young families to their service. Often, however, the agenda is less about a genuine desire to serve these families, and see them grow in their discipleship, than a desire for the existing church to gain from their presence and create an atmosphere that feels (whatever the reality) more lively and relevant.

The key factor here (and one especially relevant to the question of how Messy Church and similar projects can lead to discipleship) is the extent to which the churches themselves are prepared to change in order to facilitate the addition of new families. It was Vincent Donovan who said that growing disciples is less about Christians coming alongside people so that they can 'become like us' than about Christians coming alongside people so that they can travel together to that new place where God wants them to be.[2] Discipleship is, of course, a lifelong journey of 'learning Christ' for all believers. The most effective means of encouraging it among newcomers to the church is to meet them with a culture that combines a warm welcome with the strong sense that everyone, however long they have been Christians, is seeking to be taken by God to somewhere new.

Harshly put, building an effective strategy for encouraging discipleship might mean that churches which have planted Messy Churches have to ask uncomfortable questions about why the new venture was needed in the first place. Sometimes the answer is that a meeting time different from the normal Sunday service (typically a late afternoon midweek or a Saturday) has been identified as the best opportunity to attract the target grouping. More often, however, it is that the existing congregation have been unwilling or unable to make the changes to their Sunday service that are necessary to attract those being targeted by Messy Church.

Perhaps through necessity, the weakness within many fresh expressions of church is that they are bolted on to the side of an existing church that remains otherwise largely unchanged. This weakness is often less apparent when connections with newcomers are first being established by Messy Church. It becomes more so once a strategy for encouraging ongoing discipleship among these newcomers is needed, chiefly due to the lack of infrastructure to facilitate it. Regular churchgoers often have a good deal to encourage their retention and growth, besides the church service they attend—most obviously, smaller midweek groups and social events. But the frequent lack of integration of Messy Church into an overall missional strategy within the planting church means that such supports are less obviously available to newcomers.

The other tough question that needs asking, when the issue of Messy Church and discipleship is addressed, is 'How much genuine discipleship actually exists within more traditional congregations?' The desire to see people grow in their faith and discipleship is crucial, but sometimes more is expected of newcomers in this regard than of the church's existing members. A great deal of regular churchgoing is habitual, and, even within the most outwardly dynamic churches, the assumption needs to be challenged that long-term attendance necessarily results in the growth of discipleship. In reality, the level of really committed discipleship in established churches of all traditions is quite low, with 80% of the work in these churches still being done by 20% of the congregation. The low level of commitment may be disguised by the fact that the 80% of members not pulling their weight are nonetheless comfortable within the prevailing culture of the church, and well practised in its way of speaking and acting (sometimes known as its 'vernacular').

In saying this, I am not trying to encourage cynicism about established churches. The point is simply that making genuine disciples of Jesus Christ is a challenge for all forms of church, not just fresh expressions such as Messy Church—and this perspective is needed when the progress and success of such projects is being assessed.

What all of this means is that an overall strategy regarding discipleship for a church is usually required if its attached Messy Church is to develop sustained disciples (learners) of Jesus Christ. The strategy will result in an approach that seeks to identify the next stage of discipleship for every major grouping within the church, rather than simply its newcomers. Such a church will be aiming to meet all of its members 'where they are', but with the corollary that every member is also being challenged to grow further towards being the person whom God made them to be. Once this occurs, the church will experience a lessening of the sense of 'them and us' in regard to those encountered by Messy Church, and the programme working towards this overall aim will serve the members of Messy Church and the development of their discipleship much more effectively.

In a moment, we will consider what the elements of that programme might look like. But before that, it is instructive to remember that the challenge of making disciples from fresh expressions such as Messy Church is far from new. From very early in the history of Christianity, fresh expressions of church were being planted as Paul and others proclaimed the gospel of Jesus Christ to pagan Gentiles and founded new communities of very different Christians around the Mediterranean. The initial stages of such mission were tough but relatively simple: the good news of Jesus Christ was proclaimed and, despite a good deal of opposition and rejection, many people responded. The point at which the mission became more complex and heart-rending for Paul was when questions were raised about the continued discipleship of these Gentile Christians within the church, not least because it involved the vital issue of how these newer members related to the existing members of the more established churches as one united body.

For Paul, this question was crucial. There was no possibility that he would encourage his Gentile Christian communities to grow in their discipleship independently of the more established Jewish churches. Part of the valid critique mounted against fresh expressions by the likes of Andrew Davison and Alison Milbank focuses on the weak ecclesiology (theological understanding of the church) that appears to present the modern equivalent of this division between communities as an option.[3] Presumably it was just as tempting for Paul as it is for modern exponents of fresh expressions to develop the discipleship of new converts independently of more established believers, with all their potentially off-putting cultural baggage. If Paul had done so, however, it would have been a denial of the truth at the heart of the gospel—that God acts in Jesus Christ to bring people from every race, background and culture into his one united people.

Galatians is the letter in which Paul demonstrates that any form of apartheid between Jewish and Gentile Christians is a straightforward denial of the gospel. But it is within Paul's letters to the Romans and Ephesians that we see the clearest examples of the inextricable connection between this ecclesiology and the theme of discipleship.[4] Both letters include lengthy sections focused on discipleship (Romans 12—15; Ephesians 4—6), probably representing the major purpose for which these letters were written. But in both cases, the practical instructions on discipleship are integrated with a preceding and detailed theological explanation of the united people of God, to which both the established Jewish Christians and the newcomer Gentile Christians now belong together. Romans in particular (but possibly Ephesians as well) was written to a church where there was a very clear danger that Jewish and Gentile Christians would exist separately from one another, and the reason for Paul's detailed exposition is to show that the climax of God's covenant with Israel was always intended to be the incorporation of the Gentiles within his one united people. The challenge that Romans therefore holds out to both its Jewish and Gentile recipients is to recognise the non-negotiability of their single identity; to fully accept and love their brothers and sisters in Christ (including their differences); and to work out the practicalities of what it means to be a follower of Jesus Christ within this ecclesiological context.

A similar vision is needed if we are to respond to the challenge that Messy Church has presented in terms of growing disciples. The thousands of Messy Churches planted up and down the country are, in many ways, the equivalent of the small Gentile communities that were planted in far-flung places like Cyprus, Lystra, Philippi and Ephesus, and there is no reason to suppose that any of the challenges in drawing newcomers from a pagan culture into committed and permanent Christian discipleship were any less challenging in Paul's time than they are today. But the answer lies in taking just as seriously as Paul did the gospel principle that such discipleship, for both newcomers and established believers, can only be worked out effectively within the single people of God.

The originators of Messy Church are certainly aware of the need to develop ongoing discipleship. Many of the thoughts that they have produced about this issue, and the resources that they have made available, are really excellent.[5] Their strengths include close attention to the number of different ways in which people learn, and a recognition of the need to build discipleship programmes that seek to take people forward one step at a time. They further include the importance of acting within, rather than away from, the God-given desire for community, creativity and celebration that has brought people to Messy Church in the first place.

What needs to be added, however, if the pioneering work of Messy Church is going to result in committed discipleship, is integration within a body of Christ where *all* of its members are challenged to be transformed by what happens when God adds to their number. Some readers will have already noticed the influence of the so-called 'new perspective on St Paul' upon the thinking in this chapter. This movement within biblical scholarship began with the publication of *Paul and Palestinian Judaism* by Ed Sanders in 1977, but it has undergone considerable refinement by other scholars and contains a great deal of diversity.[6] One of the foremost gains of the new perspective has been its recognition of the centrality of ecclesiology for Paul: at the heart of his theology and understanding of the gospel was the very practical issue of how Jewish Christians and Gentile Christians developed together within one church.

It is now the task of practitioners to work out how these insights from the new perspective can be applied to the current context of church life. Just one example of its relevance is the extent to which it informs the question of how established Christians and those produced by fresh expressions such as Messy Church should relate to one another. Close examination of the way Paul responds to the issues of Christian growth within the 'mixed economy' of a Jewish and Gentile church suggests the following priorities when we are seeking to develop discipleship:

- teaching both newcomers and established Christians how God is bringing 'Messy disciples' into his one, united people
- the encouragement of oneness and mutual blessing through symbolic and practical actions
- the reshaping of the church to make relevant discipleship more central

The probable context of Paul's letter to the Romans was problems with relationships between Jewish and Gentile Christians within the Roman church. Emperor Claudius had ordered the expulsion of Jews from Rome around AD49, and one of the effects of this would have been the domination of the Roman church by Gentile Christians for a number of years before the return of the Jewish Christians. Writing sometime after their return, in the second half of the 50s, Paul is faced with actual or potential separation between these groupings, possibly fuelled by the tendencies that eventually grew into Marcionism, the second-century heresy that attempted to eliminate anything Jewish from Christianity. His response is an exposition of the biblical narrative designed to demonstrate that God's covenant with Israel was always intended to reach its climax in Jesus' arrival as Israel's Messiah, *precisely in order to bring the Gentiles, alongside the Jews, into his one united family*.

Jewish Christians are therefore called to rejoice at the entry of the Gentiles because it represents the fulfilment of Israel's story and the purpose of their calling, while Gentile Christians are called to show love and gratitude towards the Jews for preserving the inheritance that they are now receiving. It is from this basis, and with the greatest possible emphasis upon their interrelatedness and the need to love and bear with one another, that both the Jewish and Gentile Christians of Rome are then called to an ongoing life of radical discipleship.

Something very similar is needed in our current context if the 'Jewish Christians' within established congregations and the 'Gentiles' of Messy Church are going to be summoned to a common path of growth and discipleship. Of course, there is a uniqueness about both Israel's role in God's covenant plan and that crucial first-century moment when Gentiles entered the church, but the parallels with contemporary issues surrounding established churches and fresh expressions are too compelling to ignore. They point to the need for the provision of a similar narrative within which newcomers and longer-term Christians can locate themselves. Messy Church newcomers need to hear that, in becoming followers of Jesus Christ, they are joining the single family of God on completely equal terms with established Christians. But they also need to be encouraged to be grateful towards those longer-term members of God's people who have preserved the legacy that they are now receiving. Equally important is the need for more established Christians, at the churches that have planted a Messy Church, to be supplied with a narrative that shows God constantly working to bring in outsiders, on completely equal terms, into one united church.

In both cases, and in a manner appropriate to each, newcomers and established members need to be taught about the radical and unprecedented act of reconciliation that God brought about in the first century, and helped to recognise their own place within its ongoing implementation.

However, it is not enough merely to state this oneness of the church that 'Messy disciples' are entering. Any genuine ecclesiology will be reflected and reinforced by symbolic and practical actions. This is where the sacraments play a crucial role.[7] Oneness can be displayed particularly when a baptism takes place at Messy Church. On these occasions, if at all possible, members of the church that has planted the Messy Church should be warmly invited, with a priority placed on ensuring that some attend as a powerful symbol that God is adding to the number of his one united church.

Holy Communion is intended to play a similar unifying role, but its restriction within most churches to those who have been baptised (at least) means that it will be less able to represent unity in this context. Where a great deal of the power of the first-century practice of the Lord's Supper can be experienced, however, is in a shared meal, where the local but diverse members of God's single family come together to celebrate their oneness in Jesus Christ. Like the Alpha course before it, Messy Church has brilliantly rediscovered the communal power created by eating together, but this can and should be extended further. Established members of the planting church should be regularly invited to attend the Messy Church celebration and meal to enjoy fellowship with their new brothers and sisters, with the latter then invited back to a shared meal hosted by the established congregation.

Much of the theological foundation for this symbolic praxis will be bolstered by rediscovering the firmly ecclesiological nature of the doctrine of justification by faith. As Tom Wright has shown, this doctrine emerged within the context of Christians who were seeking to determine with whom they should sit down to eat, as brothers and sisters.[8] Paul's answer is that table fellowship should and must apply to all those marked out (or 'justified') as God's people by their faith in Jesus Christ. But alongside table fellowship, another vital sign of this ecclesiological truth was the financial collection that Paul organised among the Gentile churches for the relief of the starving church in Jerusalem. Paul refers to this collection several times within his letters and spells out its significance when he says, 'For if the Gentiles have shared in the Jews' spiritual blessings, they owe it to the Jews to share with them their material blessings' (Romans 15:27).

It is clear that this 'service of the saints', with its emphasis on the mutual blessing involved in being part of the single people of God, was core to the discipleship that Paul was encouraging.

Making disciples through Messy Church will involve actively seeking opportunities to encourage a similar mutual blessing between newcomers and established Christians. One of the most obvious ways of doing this would be by encouraging the people coming to Messy Church to visit older members of the planting church and support them with tasks such as shopping, transport or gardening. Often, this is best done by linking up people who live near one another. When the links are made and genuine relationships are formed, the blessings eventually flow both ways. Newer disciples start to learn, through their service, what it means 'to lose your life for Jesus and the gospel in order to find it', and perhaps discover more about 'treasure in jars of clay' as they see older Christians persevering with God through the hardships and disappointments of their lives. Older disciples learn more about the blessings that always come upon God's people when they welcome, with joy and gratitude, the newcomers whom he is calling to belong to him, and when they are open to the surprising ways in which God acts.

In both cases, these experiences need to be built upon and inter-preted by appropriate teaching that spells out the theology of what is occurring. Newcomers need to be provided with a Christian explanation of why they have received such a buzz from their self-giving, and established members need to be encouraged to recognise the blessings that are always given to insiders like Naomi (the Israelite) when God takes in outsiders like Ruth (the Gentile Moabite).

The really crucial factor that is required for ongoing disciples to be produced from Messy Church is that the planting church itself should change and be reshaped. As mentioned, many Messy Churches are bolted on to the side of churches that remain largely unchanged. When this is the case, it is very difficult for the fresh expression to grow ongoing disciples, especially once the life situations of its members move them beyond the circumstances that originally attracted them. Also, most Messy Churches meet just once a month, which inhibits discipleship, not least because missing a session results in significant discontinuity. The success of many fresh expressions of church in attracting newcomers can sometimes disguise the number of these people who later slip away. My conviction is that ongoing discipleship is most likely to occur through the integration of newcomers into the planting church.

Resistance to this idea often comes from the strongest advocates of fresh expressions, who frequently want them to be seen as churches in their own right. Their concern is that the new and exciting ways of 'doing church' that have attracted newcomers will be quashed if these people are then expected to conform to cultural patterns that are alien to them. This fear is completely legitimate, but the correct response is an insistence that churches change to incorporate the newer members. This will not be simply for the good of the newcomers, because providing more fully the elements that attracted them in the first place will also bring much greater energy to the existing members of the church as well. In the case of Messy Church, there are very few churches where most of their members would not benefit from an increased emphasis upon creativity, community and all-age provision. This does not mean that every service should be in the style of Messy Church. However, if an attached Messy Church has attracted newcomers, it does mean that *some* services should be in the new style, and that at least one regular service should be only one or two steps removed from it.

Once again, the model can be seen in what happened in the early church through the incorporation of the Gentiles. Initially, led by the Holy Spirit, this mission just happened, but there came a point when the church had to recognise what the Spirit was doing and change accordingly (Acts 8; 10—11; 13—15). Rather than simply coexisting as separate churches, the centrality of ecclesiology to the gospel of Jesus Christ compelled the one church to reinvent itself as a Jews-plus-Gentiles body. This was challenging but also incredibly energising and productive for the whole church—just one example being how much of the New Testament scripture that we possess was produced directly through Spirit-led reflection upon how the reinvention should be accomplished. In fact, Christian theology itself was born through this very process.[9]

Messy Church has blazed a trail that is similar to the early Gentile mission. Very many people have been wonderfully touched by God's grace. But it is now time for the established churches to change in order to welcome these brothers and sisters, so that we can go forward together as one church. To repeat, this is not just for the sake of the newcomers. As the church responds to this challenge, it will discover a more relevant form of discipleship within our current world for all of its members. All Christians face the danger that our faith will eventually become escapism, and it is the influx of new members that makes biblical engagement with the real issues of the contemporary world inescapable. The one church desperately needs the fresh and exciting (re)discovery of creativity, community and all-age Christianity that Messy Church has made in responding to this world. Responding to Messy Church itself and other fresh expressions of church with a biblical ecclesiology is now essential for all of us if we are to move forward in our ongoing calling to be lifelong disciples of Jesus Christ.

MISSIONAL STRUCTURES FOR MISSIONAL OUTCOMES

Messy Church, nodality, modality and sodality, and the kingdom of God

Tim Dakin became Bishop of Winchester in December 2011. He was previously General Secretary / Executive Leader of the Church Mission Society now based in Oxford. Prior to that he was Principal of Carlile College in Nairobi. He has an East African background but was educated mostly in England. He is married with two grown-up children.

This chapter sets Messy Church in the wider context of both the priority of mission engagement, which is a priority for Messy Church, and of new expressions of mission-shaped church, of which Messy Church is an example. It suggests that for mission to be a priority, and for the church to refresh the expression of its missional nature, three dynamic structures are needed.[1] First, we need **visionary mission leadership** in the apostolic tradition (nodality),[2] which coordinates the two other dynamics of complementary missional church: **parish-neighbourhood expressions** (modality) and **network-focused expressions** (sodality).[3] Messy Church may be seen as a sodal movement enabling fresh expressions of sodal or modal church. The threefold ecology is aimed at sustaining holistic discipleship shaped by Jesus' mission of the kingdom of God.

Thus mission is here understood as God's active intention both to complete and to restore creation as the kingdom of God. The kingdom of God is the milieu of God's action, his reign, in which he shares his life with us, inviting us to discover fullness of life by participating in his mission of fulfilling the kingdom.[4] The revelation of this plan is focused in Jesus, who enacts God's kingdom in his life, death and resurrection, and by his ongoing mission through the Spirit.[5] The outworking of this mission is a world-affirming, world-transforming discipleship of living the mission of Jesus, inspired and enabled by the power of the Spirit.[6] The church is missional in so far as it is grounded and shaped by the lived expression of God's mission.[7] Ensuring that the church remains missional requires constant reshaping and occasional refounding.[8]

In the Diocese of Winchester in the Church of England we have clarified the meaning of these terms. I hope that these definitions might be useful for other denominations, just as Messy Church works across the traditions.[9]

- **Modality** comes from the word 'mode', meaning the customary way things are done. A modal expression of church is one that is locally rooted, in which there is no distinction by ethnicity, sex or age and in which there may be a great variation of commitment and a wide-ranging approach to mission. Classically, for Anglicans, the parish and deanery are expressions of modality. However, fresh expressions of modal church are emerging across the denominations, and Messy Church can be a fresh expression of modality.

- **Sodality** comes from the Latin root *sodalis*, which can be translated as 'companion'. It implies partnership for a common purpose. A sodal expression of church often includes a second-level commitment beyond church membership or baptismal promises; it might be limited by age, sex or marital status, and tends to be a more mobile expression of missional church, focused on its mission or ministry task. Sodalities are also sometimes characterised by a commitment to work beyond the normal cultural and contextual boundaries of a church, establishing new Christian communities. The religious orders and mission societies are traditional expressions of sodality, although fresh expressions of religious and mission societies are now also emerging as new monastic, friarly or missional communities, and Messy Church could be included as one of these.

- **Nodality** is leadership that promotes mission engagement and encourages the collaboration, growth and development of both modal and sodal expressions of missional church and their respective licensed ministries (including pioneers). It encourages their involvement in a range of mission, reflecting a whole-life vision of the kingdom of God—for example, evangelism, social enterprise, family life and work, and education.

The missional turn

It seems that everything has become missionary, missional or mission-shaped! There has been a missional turn—particularly in the West—in our understanding of God, Christian life and the church.[10] In the West we have been brought up short by the decline of Christianity and the realisation that the Western world is now just as much a mission field as anywhere else. In fact, the heartlands of Christianity are now found in the southern hemisphere, and missionaries are coming from there to the West.[11]

The missional turn is only partially stimulated by this decline. A major stimulant of the missional turn is, in fact, the growing impact of the missional culture of global Christianity. The irony is that modern global Christianity has arisen, largely, as a result of the initial mission activity of Western Christianity. As Andrew Walls notes, Christian presence ebbs and flows from different contexts, although the globalisation of Christianity now puts mission in a new framework.[12]

What is now needed is a new evangelisation within Western culture and a new missiology to go with it.[13] I am suggesting that we also need missional structures and missional outcomes. The Church of England has responded to this challenge. The *Mission-shaped Church* report[14] has had a major impact on the imagination and practice of the church, resulting in initiatives like Fresh Expressions and the development of lay and ordained pioneer ministers. The Messy Church movement is part of this kind of development, making a significant contribution to the church's outreach. Crucially, Messy Church connects well with those who are de-churched but open to faith, as well as with non-churched people.[15] Messy Church has also spread across the denominations, becoming an interdenominational mission initiative.

Messy Church is part of a missional church

Messy Church is one movement that helps us to see the need to prioritise mission engagement, but is there a more radical change taking place? I believe that Messy Church illustrates a wider change: there is a 'refounding' taking place of Christian mission to the West, one rooted in a wider and deeper understanding of God's mission in which we are invited to participate now and for eternity. This refounding is both a recovery and a lived-out interpretation of the mission of Jesus for today.

In the diocese where I serve as Diocesan Bishop, there are currently about 50 Messy Churches. Paul Moore, cofounder with Lucy Moore of the first Messy Church, writes that the aim of Messy Church is 'to be an all-age expression of Church for those who are not used to going to church (not a bridge into Sunday church), and to be a Christ-centred community where adults and children can encounter Jesus and grow in faith'.[16] There are now over 3500 registered Messy Churches across the world. There are also numerous initiatives that make use of insights from Messy Church without being registered as such.

Many of these Messy Churches and initiatives share a common DNA, with four aspects: hospitality, creativity, all-age, and celebration. George Lings sees each of these being given structure and shape by the overall Christ-centred character of Messy Church. To this I would add the need for there to be a kingdom outcome as the other strand of the DNA of Messy Church, running parallel with Christ-centredness.[17]

In exploring the nature of Messy Church, Paul Moore reviews how the four classic marks of the Church translate into Messy Church culture:

Messy Church is 'apostolic' in the way it continues the mission of the risen Lord; it is 'one' in the way it emphasises relationship and unity in diversity; Messy Church is also part of the wider universal, 'catholic' people of God; and, finally, becoming 'holy' is the focus of Messy Church's transformational worship, where the sacraments are also foundational.[18] In the missional vision of credal Christianity, the Holy Spirit inspires this fourfold shape of the church. We could therefore see in Messy Church the dynamic equivalent of what has traditionally been recognised as the one, holy, catholic and apostolic Church, centred on Christ, inspired by the Spirit in the life of the kingdom of God the Father.

Sending and receiving: beyond territorial Christianity

The impact of spatial language—'from here to there'—on our understanding of mission has been, and still is, considerable. We need to tease out how mission as 'sending' can have a number of meanings. Sending can mean a physical movement of going somewhere at the behest of another person. It can also refer to something like sending a message, sharing communication with others and developing a relationship of receiving as well as sending. This is a vision for a quality of relationships marked by peace. The deeper form of sending is implied by the vision of mission in John's Gospel: 'Jesus said to them again, "Peace be with you. As the Father has sent me, so I send you." When he had said this, he breathed on them and said to them, "Receive the Holy Spirit"' (John 20:21–22, NRSV). Jesus draws his disciples into the great mission of God—to become like God in his mission (the analogy of mission).

The globalisation of mission, where everywhere is a place of sending and receiving, begins to recast mission in relational terms and highlights the importance of local sending and local communication. It also begins to highlight the importance of how sending happens, the way in which sending and receiving take place—the quality of the sharing, the depth of mutuality, the multiple layers of sharing, and the collaborative and cooperative structures needed for mission engagement to remain flexible and to develop. As Andrew Walls notes:

> The territorial 'from–to' idea that underlay the older missionary movement has to give way to a concept much more like that of the Christians within the Roman Empire in the second and third centuries: parallel presences in different circles and different levels each seeking to penetrate within and beyond its circle.[19]

One of the ways in which this multilayered and mutually collaborative approach can be developed is through the threefold ecology proposed in this chapter; enabled by mission leadership, the sodality and modality can work together in a new and enriched model of contextual mission engagement.

Modality, sodality and nodality

Stephen B. Bevans and Roger Schroeder suggest that in the Acts of the Apostles we see seven stages of mission. In each new stage the church adapts to a new form of mission and is changed by that adaptation: 'as the mission takes shape, so does the church'.[20] From these changes a question arises: what resources these new forms of mission and what helps the church to adapt to new mission and incorporate changes into church life? One way of answering this might be to look at the theology—the worldview and way of life—of the emerging new and different approaches to mission and church. In fact, Bevans and Schroeder do just that: they explore six underlying theological constants that are reworked as new mission contexts are engaged (Christology, ecclesiology, salvation, eschatology, anthropology and culture) and they propose three theological styles that have appeared over the centuries (initially associated with Carthage, Alexandria and Antioch, the key categories for each being law, truth and history respectively), which resource new mission. However, this kind of resource points to another—the human resource that develops this missional reflection and uses it to guide the Christian movement into further expansion.[21]

Another way of looking at the question of what underlies change in mission and church is to ask whether there is a mission structure that persists through the various stages of mission and in the shape of church. Using a model first proposed by Ralph Winter (in *The Two Structures of God's Redemptive Mission*)—but here expanded to include perspectives from Craig Van Gelder (in *Local and Mobile: A study of two functions*[22])—I propose that there are three structural elements to the dynamics of mission and that they take form in the church and shape the church. These three elements are 'modal' church, bonding people together locally; 'sodal' church, bridging to different places and peoples to create new community; and 'nodal' mission leadership, linking modal and sodal but also ensuring that the outcomes and impact of mission engage with gospel issues about the fullness of life. These three elements are the mission capital by which the Christian movement develops and by which the church is shaped. Together they enable the *telos* of mission—the unfolding dynamic of all things being united in Christ.

Prioritising mission requires constant engagement and adaptation. It might also mean that the church is a little bit messy in itself as it changes in response to mission developments. In the Church of England we might identify three great shifts: the English Reformation, the reorganisation of dioceses and the Modern Mission Movement. All these were part of wider social changes, the first as part of great upheavals in British society and culture, the second as part of the reform of social institutions in the 19th century,[23] and the third reflecting the extensive European migrations that took place from the 17th century onwards and whose outworking continues today in mission and globalisation. However, the third shift also represents a mission-shift in the church's self-understanding, which emerged in the global mission initiatives of the mission societies but is now beginning to be fully integrated into the rest of the wider church through the language of mission-shaped church and the missional nature of church. It is this mission dynamic that I am exploring here, relating it to Messy Church and the kingdom of God.

I am therefore suggesting that there is a structural dynamic which enables the recognition of new mission and the church's adaptation to new mission. I've proposed that there are three elements in this dynamic: nodality, sodality and modality. The first, nodality, is the apostolic leadership that recognises and prioritises the movement of God's mission and also shapes the response to opportunities, coordinating the other two elements of sodality and modality in each context. The other two elements, sodality and modality, embody in Christian communities two principles of mission: the pilgrimage and indigenisation principles, respectively. The first engages the wider culture and unreached elements of human society; the second emphasises specific expressions of faith in local communities. This threefold dynamic is essential to the vitality and flexibility of the Christian movement. Together they enable holistic evangelisation and ongoing conversion, expressing the kingdom of God in the life of the world.[24]

Ralph Winter was one of the first to suggest that a differentiation in the life of mission and the church was essential to the vitality of both mission and the church. Winter refers to modality and sodality as two aspects of God's mission and therefore two structural elements in the church. These two dimensions can be traced from the start of Christianity all the way through to the present day.

The first expression of these two structures in the New Testament period can be seen in the emergence of local congregations, such as the one in Corinth ('modal'), and the activities of the mobile mission bands led by people like Paul ('sodal'). In the centuries that followed, both dynamics of church life continued, but at times there was a tense relationship between the local church, in the form of the diocese and parish, and the various forms of mobile church, such as the monastic movement, the preaching orders and the friars. Both forms of church could be missional and bring new life to mission, and both could undermine Christian mission. Both forms were also accountable to some sort of overarching leadership, such as the Pope, and both contributed to the development of mission.[25] Cooperating together under mission leadership (nodality), these two forms (modality and sodality) generate and enable the vision, communities and social outworking of the gospel.

The Protestant Reformation saw the emergence of new forms of local congregations but did not see the emergence of equivalent sodalities until the mission societies developed.[26] Before this, the Roman Catholic response to the Reformation did include new mission communities, such as the Jesuits. I believe that both forms of missional church are necessary but both need an external point of leadership and direction that is not part of either—missional symbiosis enabled by mission leadership.[27]

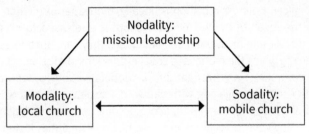

Diagram 1

It would be important to recognise here that Messy Church is not necessarily sodal, but only where it functions strongly as a new mission community engaging with a cross-cultural or new contextual challenge. This form of Messy Church would require other sodal characteristics, such as a second-level commitment and a pioneering leadership that keeps a clear focus for the community.[28]

Modality and sodality are complementary expressions of missional church. Indeed, for there to be effective mission, both dimensions are needed. Each can help renew the other and there can be fresh expressions of both the sodal and the modal. Winter argues that the great advantage of the Roman Catholic use of the modal and the sodal was the synthesis they achieved between the two; he describes these two dimensions as the 'warp and the woof'. But the question arises:

what keeps these two dimensions together and what guides them in mission? Winter does not answer this question, even though the answer was implied in his appreciation of the Roman Catholic synthesis. It lies in there being a third kind of dynamic and structure—a missional authority or leadership that provides a directional oversight and focus of unity in mission. Van Gelder develops an implicit model of this third dynamic and structure, but does not explore it further. He recognises the place of the Bible, the Pope and the diocese, but leaves his analysis there rather than exploring missional leadership—the apostolic dynamic, office and function—as something to be incorporated into missional theology.[29]

In Anglican polity, the bishop is, ideally, the leader of mission and also the focus of unity.[30] Where bishops are released to exercise this double role (with other senior leaders) they can function as the means by which the modal and sodal expressions of mission, ministry and community are brought into a cooperative and collaborative relationship for engaging with and within society and culture. This kind of mission leadership therefore becomes an essential element in defining what is ecclesial and how missional church is fostered; it can be called the nodality.[31] As Arbuckle illustrates with reference to the Roman Catholic Church, the re-establishing of sodalities is hard work and requires the support of the hierarchy,[32] but, again, ideally it would be good if the apostolic responsibility of nodalities consciously included responsibility for supporting sodal and modal mission.[33]

Some might argue that the episcopal function is shared by everyone. Famously, Thomas Torrance suggests that there is a corporate episcopate in which all church members share.[34] Much of what Torrance says can be affirmed—that we all share in a common baptism, that some are set aside for a priesthood relating to the word and sacrament, and that from among that priesthood some exercise a particular ministry of oversight of the whole body. Nevertheless, the insight which the episcopal tradition maintains is that the bishop has an *apostolic* responsibility that draws on Jesus' mission leadership and his commission to the disciples. It is the missional nature of episcopacy that Torrance misses. This is distinct but is nevertheless shared by the bishop with others and, indeed, enabled in the whole people of God. The nodality of the bishop is missional and is for the mission of all to, and in, all the world.

McNair-Scott identifies three types of apostolic leadership (canonical, coordinating and corporate).[35] In all three, apostolic leadership is shaped by the priority of keeping mission engagement to the fore and enabling mission to happen through collaborative communities of action; and all three are found in nodal missional leadership. Nodality is foundational in that it has an authority that reflects the significance of the original apostles (canonical). But it is also hierarchical in coordinating the ministry in local churches, ensuring cooperation between roles, gifts and responsibilities (as in the Ephesians 4 list of apostles, prophets, evangelists and pastor-teachers). Lastly, it can also move about between members; it is corporate, according to need.

Within Anglican polity, all these three aspects are focused in the personal episcopacy of the diocesan bishop—but they are also shared with the College of Presbyters and through diocesan synodical governance. The office of the bishop is therefore essential, personal, shared and corporate.[36]

Messy Church as church

Messy Church can be an extension of existing forms of modal church or can become a new expression of church that is recognised as being ecclesial in its own right. A Messy Church approach can also be the basis for a sodal missional community, in so far as it is cross-cultural or is addressing new contextual challenges so that it may also be recognised as a different sort of church in its own right.

The team around George Lings has suggested ten questions for recognising a fresh expression of church:[37]

1 Is it a new group which is Christian and communal?
2 Does the group aim to engage with non-churchgoers?
3 Does it meet at least once a month?
4 Does it have a name?
5 Does it intend to be church?
6 Is it an Anglican or ecumenical project with an Anglican partner?
7 Is there some form of recognised leadership?
8 Do the majority of members see this as their main expression of being church?
9 Are there aspirations to express the four classic marks of church: one, holy, catholic, apostolic?
10 Is there an intention to become self-supporting, self-governing and self-reproducing?[38]

These ten questions are intended to expand on four major foundational characteristics for identifying a fresh expression of church, while challenging existing churches: it engages with non-churchgoers (missional); it fits the context (contextual); it aims to form disciples (formational); and it intends to be church (ecclesial).

The responsibility of nodal leadership is to encourage and recognise fresh expressions of both modal and sodal missional church. Here, the Messy Church movement makes a significant contribution as one that enables modal church to be more missional, contextual, formational and ecclesial. This can lead to new expressions or refreshed expressions of modal church.[39] The question for the Messy Church movement is whether it wants to be recognised as church within a given denomination or remain as an ecumenical sodality that sits alongside denominations, resourcing them in their mission initiatives.

This question may become sharper if Messy Churches within a denomination are recognised as ecclesial communities in their own right and yet the wider movement itself is seen not as fully ecclesial (as above) but as a resource ministry. Here the role of nodal mission leadership may be important in mediating between a wider movement and the adaptation of that movement's resources within a denominational ecclesiology. It is not uncommon for Anglican bishops to play this role, ensuring recognition and take-up of a movement's ministry.

Messy Church and the challenge of the kingdom

One of the key responsibilities of the nodality is to ensure that both the modal and the sodal are oriented beyond themselves—in other words, that their priorities go beyond maintaining their church and reach out to non-Christians, supporting broader aspects of Christian witness in local community and wider society.[40] This means understanding that the outcome of ministry and the formation of the Christian community are best seen from the standpoint of the Christian as citizen, witnessing in the wider world.[41]

Crucial here is not just the missional vitality of the church, but also the nature of mission; it is grounded in Jesus' mission of the kingdom of God, a social reality that includes both the creational and redemptive dimensions of God's action in the world. However, if Jesus' mission of the kingdom becomes just a metaphor or a cypher for extending and growing the church as a religious institution, then the church has usurped the place of the kingdom. The mission of Jesus is the gospel of the kingdom. The mission leadership of Jesus is his prophetic expression of this life, drawing on and fulfilling the narrative of Israel, and inviting people into the hope that one day the whole world would be drawn into the kingdom of God. It is through the combination of the mission of both the sodal and modal dynamics, coordinated by nodal mission leadership, that the outcome of discipleship in the-world-as-the-kingdom-of-God can be enabled.

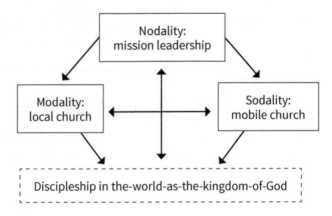

Diagram 2

So, having earlier noted George Lings' reflections on the DNA of Messy Church, I want here to highlight another general feature which is a key element of Messy Church—its world-affirming and world-transforming culture. Messy Church's 'Yes' to the kingdom of God as the Christian life-world is theologically strategic: kingdom is the practical interpretation of living in the wider world that we share with others.

In the trilogy of books on Messy Church by Lucy Moore—who is leader of what has now become the Messy Church movement—there is an implicit world-affirming and world-transforming expression of mission and church.[42] It is easy to miss this aspect by reducing the creative aspects of its DNA to arts and crafts activities. Yet in the double helix of Messy Church DNA, it is the 'Yes' to the life of the kingdom, running parallel to Christ-centredness, which holds together the four aspects of hospitality, creativity, all-age and celebration. In *Messy Church 3* (p. 22), Lucy writes about the impact that Messy Church can have on the vitality of Christianity in a difficult context:

> Whatever the future holds, you are part of the happy band of intrepid explorers hacking a path through the wilderness with scissors, double-sided sticky tape and glitter glue. You are helping children and adults today and tomorrow to find their way to the

goodness of God and enjoy the life-changing benefits of being citizens of his kingdom.

Sometimes it is the small but habitual actions that change both a personal perspective and a community culture, thereby opening up a wider view of the world and how to live in it. Messy Church is about this sort of activity. Small creative acts, when done in the perspective of Christ's presence and with the vision of the kingdom and in the company of others, can mean so much more than might be expected. This kind of practising of life-world knowledge, of lived wisdom, is a powerful means of wider change. The empowerment to live the mission of Jesus, by the Holy Spirit, is the starting point for this perspective.[43]

In his mission, Jesus reminds people of the good news that God wants to share his life with creation and wants to do that with all people, beginning with Israel. The mission of Jesus shows us what this looks like—God's life shared with us and our life shared with him in the kingdom of God. Therefore, one way of talking about the kingdom of God is as the space in which God shares his life with created existence. Messy Church is one way of exploring how to understand this at a practical and shared level with others.

Messy Church discipleship and culture

A key challenge for Messy Church is to encourage this low-key involvement to develop and to overflow into a wider mission engagement with family, school, work, social enterprise and a Christian citizenship that is committed to contributing to the common good. Messy Church projects are already experimenting with some of these wider domains of life, but it might be interesting if Messy Church were encouraged deliberately to engage with a particular domain, such as an after-school club, a foodbank or a Citizens Advice bureau. This might make it more like a sodality than a fresh expression of modal church.

A wider vision for mission challenges the notion that faith is limited to the personal life or confined to a particular social domain, such as a religious institution or Sunday church. We might want to talk about different aspects of life, but everything is linked. One of the things Christian faith offers is a whole-life vision of what it means to be human, participating in the fullness of life that God offers in the kingdom.

The holistic vision is one that some popular commentators have developed, suggesting that everyone can be spiritual but not everyone needs to be religious. Building on this perspective, expectations of what Christian citizenship is about have thereby been lowered by the idea that we all have an implicit religion, or that some can practise religion vicariously on behalf of others. Yet Christianity is about making culture and not just connecting with culture. Culture is not neutral; it is formed by and also shapes faith and religion. Culture is used by groups in society, like church, to make meaning and to share meaning with others.

So I am not suggesting that Messy Church should attempt to connect with an implicit English religion;[44] rather, I am suggesting that we need the confidence to engage theologically with life and culture rather than looking for points of cultural contact. This means that discipleship is about practically witnessing to a whole-life vision in the kingdom. A practical expression of this is an understanding of vocation that is positive about the missional significance of business. Business is something good and creative, contributing to the common good of all through services and goods. Christian mission is not just about the great commission combined with the great commandments; it is also about the great work (or the 'greater works') that Jesus expected us to do in his name (John 14:12) and which God has prepared for us to do as part of his work of creation (Ephesians 2:10).[45]

African Christianity preserves something of this vision for life as a whole. It does not start with an individualised observer standpoint; rather, it recognises that we are already part of the life we experience, a personal knowledge derived by participation. Martin Nkemnkia describes this as 'African Vitalogy': 'In African thinking, the starting point is life's experience, life itself in its various forms and expressions. Life presents itself as the first transcendent reality. For the African everything is therefore life. Life is that which remains identical in every moment. Thus, "African Vitalogy".'[46]

We are in the early stages of another phase of the challenge of considering the relationship between gospel and culture,[47] and a lot more work probably needs to be done beyond a form of contextualisation which misuses the 'idea' of incarnation as a justification for 'baptising culture' or the idea that Christians merely accompany society and its culture. I would suggest that a 'missiology of life' might begin to touch on something beyond what we have, which is currently still held back by aspects of clericalism, 'churchianity' and the pull of Christendom. A reclaimed vision for life in the kingdom of God might be a place to start.

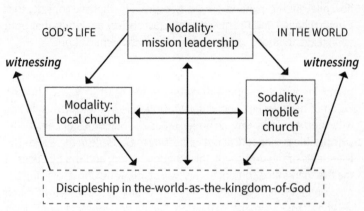

Diagram 3

God shares his life with us by becoming part of life through the mission of Jesus, revealing the kingdom of God. The incarnated life of God is the whole narrative of Jesus' mission from birth through life and ministry to his death, resurrection, ascension and glorification. It is by Jesus, as the risen, glorified mediator of life between God and creation, that we are baptised in the Holy Spirit, the Lord, the giver of life. All are thereby commissioned to live out Jesus' ongoing mission of sharing God's life with created existence. This is the kingdom of God in which all may share and find fulfilment. There is something in Messy Church that connects with this vision, but it needs to be developed further.

One practical way forward might be to explore how the vitalogy of the Messy Church movement relates to the practical way of life that goes with the five marks of mission: safeguarding and stewarding creation; transforming unjust society; loving service of human need; teaching, baptising and nurturing believers; proclaiming the kingdom of God. These five marks provide a practical apologetic for Christian faith that can be explored and expressed in the Messy Church context. Reversing the traditional order, so beginning with the care for creation (fifth mark) and leading up to the proclamation of the kingdom (the first mark and, to many interpreters, inclusive of all the other marks), makes it clear how relevant these marks are today, especially when we consider that climate change and the question of a just society are issues that both younger generations and governments are concerned about.[48]

Using the five marks in this way, apologetically, would put the question of making and engaging with culture at the heart of Messy Church's vision of discipleship, showing how God's life in the world connects with the way Messy Church understands the outcomes of church life. Discipleship is therefore about witnessing to God's life in the world. The five marks of mission shape this kingdom vision, and the practices of the five marks give content to this way of following Christ, of living the mission of Jesus. It would be very interesting to see a Messy Church version of the five marks of mission. Such a development would offer the wider church a practical apologetic.[49]

Conclusion

Just over a century ago, the 1910 Edinburgh Missionary Conference brought delegates together from all around the world. From this conference the call went out for evangelism in every continent. In the century that followed, we saw a huge and unexpected expansion of Christianity in Africa—but we also saw the decline of Christianity in Europe. Western Christians are now in one of the most challenging contexts in the world. To bring hope and faith and love into this context is the challenge of mission and missional church.[50] Theoretical apologetics connects only with a few at a certain stage in life; practical and experiential apologetics enables all generations to learn together what it might mean to follow Jesus. Messy Church offers this, and its ministry could develop in this direction to great effect.

Messy Church is an important contribution to expressing what it might mean to make mission a priority and to do it in a way that connects with the whole of life. As such, Messy Church needs the support of the nodal missional leaders, who want to see fresh expressions of church that reach out to those who need to know and experience fullness of life. Such forms of church can be both modal and sodal and can become full expressions of church in their own right. Messy Church has already developed greatly but it could take further steps towards developing a strong 'kingdom of God' strand that expands on the whole-life vision of what it means to live the mission of Jesus in the power of the Spirit.

Messy Church is a gentle form of revitalising the church, asking about priorities and raising questions about the missional character and missional structures of the church. Messy Church is about 'being church and doing life'[51] from the perspective of God's mission in the world and into eternity. Messy Church asks the questions and allows radical answers to be developed, including what is proposed here in terms of missional structures, but also what else is needed in terms of engagement with the wider world through a life of discipleship which witnesses to the kingdom of God in all of life.

NOTES

Introduction: a church for all generations

1 For an excellent analysis of the changes in values from one generation to another, based on the work of Graham Cray, and the way they shape expectations of institutional involvement, see James Lawrence, *Engaging Generation Y* (Grove, 2012), particularly the chart on page 14.

2 So Linda Woodhead commented, in the *Church Times* on 23 January 2015, that if 'all regular Sunday worshippers disappeared overnight… the Church would remain, and its most influential activities could continue'.

3 Interestingly, this is the only occurrence in the New Testament of the verb *mathetueo*, 'to make disciples'.

4 www.archbishopofcanterbury.org/articles.php/5515/revolutionary-love-archbishop-justins-lecture-on-evangelism

5 It is worth noting, though, that this is not entirely a one-way street, as demonstrated by the renewed appeal of formal chapel services to some university students (see www.telegraph.co.uk/news/religion/12176998/Looking-for-Britains-future-leaders-Try-evensong.html). Attendance at cathedral services of worship has risen 30% in the last decade.

6 A key study in this area is Richard Bauckham (ed.), *The Gospel for All Christians* (T&T Clark, 1997). Bauckham and others argue against the previous consensus in New Testament scholarship that the Gospels were written for distinct, isolated and even rival theological and geographical communities, demonstrating not just shared belief but actual communication between Christian groups in different locations. This has vital implications for how we read the New Testament, but it also changes our paradigm for thinking about ecclesial structures and missional activity.

7 For a specific proposal about the need for apostolic, translocal leadership in contemporary mission, see the late Martin Garner's *A Call for Apostles Today* (Grove, 2007).

8 Article XIX of the 39 Articles.

9 There is an interesting parallel here with the Church of England's discussion about fresh expressions. I was a member of General Synod when the *Mission-shaped Church* report was discussed, and only after the debate did a number of us realise that the question of sacramental

practice had been completely bypassed, perhaps out of a sense of urgency of welcoming new missional paradigms.

10 On both the necessity and the limitations (practical and ecclesial) of youth congregations, see Graham Cray, *Youth Congregations and the Emerging Church* (Grove, 2002).

Messy Church in different contexts

1 Lucy Moore, *Messy Church: Fresh ideas for building a Christ-centred community* (BRF, 2006), p. 10.

2 www.freshexpressions.org.uk/about/whatis

3 www.gloucester.anglican.org/schools/jumping-fish

4 See www.churchinnovations.org/what-we-do/consulting/partnership-for-missional-church

5 R.A. Heifitz, A. Grashaw and M. Linsky, *The Practice of Adaptive Leadership* (Harvard Business Press, 2009).

6 Ronald A. Heifitz and Marty Linsky, *Leadership on the Line* (Harvard Business Review Press, 2002), p. 13.

7 Aylward Shorter, 'Inculturation: win or lose the future?' in J.A. Scherer and S.B. Bevans (eds), *New Directions in Mission and Evangelism 3* (Faith and Culture) (Orbis, 1999), p. 55.

8 Aylward Shorter, 'Inculturation in Africa—the way forward' in Stephen B. Bevans (ed.), *Mission and Culture: The Louis J. Luzbetak lectures* (Orbis, 2012), p. 100.

9 Lisa McKenzie, *Getting By: Estates, class and culture in austerity Britain* (Policy Press, 2015), p. 79.

10 Office for National Statistics census data 2011.

11 McKenzie, *Getting By*, p. 47.

12 ibid., p. 48.

13 Shorter, 'Inculturation: win or lose the future?' in Scherer and Bevans (eds), *New Directions in Mission and Evangelism 3*, p. 55.

14 Andrew F. Walls, 'The gospel as prisoner and liberator of culture' in Scherer and Bevans (eds), *New Directions in Mission and Evangelism 3*, p. 22.

15 Stephen Kuhrt, *Church Growth through the Full Welcome of Children* (Grove, 2009).

16 Ibid., pp. 11–12.

17 P.T. Ellison and P. Keifert, *Dwelling in the Word* (Church Innovations, 2011).

Messy challenges: dangers and pitfalls

1 Lesson 12 in Jerome W. Berryman, *The Complete Guide to Godly Play Volume 3: 20 Presentations for Winter* (Morehouse Education Resources, 2002).

2 See the chapter 'Messy Church and the sacraments' by Philip North, later in this book.

Making sacred spaces in Messy Church

1 Pierre Teilhard de Chardin, *The Divine Milieu* (Harper Torchbooks, 1960), p. 36.

2 Hence the title of Durkheim's key work, *The Sacred and the Profane* (Harvest, 1959).

3 R. Greaves and G.D. Chryssides, *The Study of Religion: An introduction to key ideas and methods* (Continuum, 2007), p. 219.

4 A.T. Riley, '"Renegade Durkheimianism" and the transgressive/left sacred' in J.L. Alexander and P. Smith (eds), *The Cambridge Companion to Durkheim* (Cambridge University Press, 2005).

5 G. Bartle, 'Sacred places: public places', supervised research project, School of Urban Planning, McGill University (2009), p. 4.

6 S. Collins, *The Carolingian Debate over Sacred Space* (Palgrave Macmillan, 2012), pp. 9–10.

7 Michel Foucault, 'Of other spaces: utopias and heterotopias' in *Architecture/Mouvement/Continuité* (October 1984), pp. 5–7.

8 For example, see www.fengshuisociety.org.uk.

9 Rebecca Nye, *Children's Spirituality* (Church House Publishing, 2009), p. 42.

10 Ibid., pp. 43–44.

11 Ibid., p. 45.

12 Ibid.

13 George Lings, *Seven Sacred Spaces* (Church Army, 2015).

14 Ibid., pp. 9–13.

15 Henri Nouwen, *The Way of the Heart* (DLT, 1990), p. 25.

16 Lings, *Seven Sacred Spaces*, pp. 13–17.

17 Ibid., pp. 18–20.

18 Ibid., pp. 21–22.

19 Ibid., pp. 23–25.

20 Ibid., pp. 26–30.

21 Ibid., pp. 30–32.
22 Ibid., p. 34.
23 See the chapter 'Messy Church and the sacraments' by Philip North, later in this book.
24 Lings, *Seven Sacred Spaces*, p. 17.
25 Lucy Moore, *All-Age Worship* (BRF, 2010), p. 36.
26 See the chapter 'The pastoral implications of Messy Church' by Irene Smale, later in this book.

Messy Church and the sacraments

1 Mary Douglas, *Natural Symbols* (Penguin, 1978).
2 Andrew Davison and Alison Milbank discussed some of these issues in *For the Parish* (SCM Press, 2010), which continues to be a provocative contribution to the debate and has informed my own thought.
3 Graham Tomlin, *The Widening Circle* (SPCK, 2014), p. 96.
4 See Paul McPartlan, *The Eucharist Makes the Church* (Eastern Christian Publications, 2006).
5 www.churchofengland.org/prayer-worship/worship/texts/additional-eucharistic-prayers.aspx
6 www.churchofengland.org/prayer-worship/worship/texts/additional-baptism-texts-in-accessible-language.aspx

Messy Church in a postmodern world

1 Sabrina Müller, *Fresh Expressions of Church: Beobachtungen und Interpretationen einer neuen kirchlichen Bewegung* (Theologischer Verlag Zürich, 2016).
2 Graham Cray et al., *Mission-shaped Church: Church planting and Fresh Expressions of church in a changing context* (CHP, 2004/2009).
3 Alan Smith et al., *Fresh Expressions in the Mission of the Church: Report of an Anglican-Methodist working party* (CHP, 2012).
4 See George Lings (ed.), *Messy Church Theology: Exploring the significance of Messy Church for the wider church* (BRF, 2013).
5 As the report from the Church Army's Research Unit suggests, 80% of the people involved in a fresh expression wouldn't be in another church: www.churchgrowthresearch.org.uk/UserFiles/File/Reports/churchgrowthresearch_freshexpressions.pdf.

6   See, among others, Carsten Wippermann and Isabel Magalhaes, *Milieu-handbuch: Religiöse und kirchliche Orientierungen in den Sinus-Milieus 2005* (Medien-Dienstleistungs-GmbH, 2005).

7   See Linda Woodhead, 'Introduction', in Linda Woodhead and Rebecca Catto (eds), *Religion and Change in Modern Britain* (Taylor & Francis, 2012), pp. 1ff.

8   Cray et al., *Mission-shaped Church*.

9   See ibid., pp. 1–15.

10 Müller, *Fresh Expressions of Church*.

11 See ibid, Chapter 7.4.

12 See ibid, Chapter 7.4.2.

13 Thomas Schlag, *Öffentliche Kirche: Grunddimensionen einer praktisch-theologischen Kirchentheorie* (Theologischer Verlag, 2012).

14 Sinus-Milieus is the result of 30 years of sociological research. Ulrich Becker and Horst Nowak, *Lebensweltanalyse als Neue Perspektive der Meinungs und Marketingforschung* (ESOMAR, 1981).

15 See Wippermann and Magalhaes, *Milieuhandbuch*.

16 The first Reformed Church in Switzerland that conducted a Sinus-Milieus study was in Zurich in 2012. Matthias Krieg, Roland Diethelm and Thomas Schlag, Hrsg., *Lebenswelten: Modelle kirchlicher Zukunft* (Theologischer Verlag, 2012).

17 See *SINUS: Informationen zu den Sinus-Milieus* (Heidelberg, 2011).

18 See Berthold Bodo Flaig, Thomas Meyer and Jörg Ueltzhöffer, *Alltags-ästhetik und Politische Kultur: Zur ästhetischen Dimension politischer Bildung und politischer Kommunikation* (Bonn, 1997).

19 See Krieg, Diethelm and Schlag, *Lebenswelten*, pp. 9–10.

20 Sabrina Müller, 'Fresh Expressions of Church: Eine Reise zu den Anglikanern', in Krieg, Diethelm and Schlag, *Lebenswelten*.

21 'Sinus-Meta Milieus', 8, accessed 6 January 2016: www.sinus-institut.de/veroeffentlichungen/downloads.

22 Ibid.

23 Ibid.

24 Ibid.

25 The concept of theology in Messy Church fits very much into the discussion on contextual theology. See, for example, Laurie Green, *Let's Do Theology: Resources for contextual theology*, 2. Aufl. (Mowbray, 2009), pp. 4ff.

26 Müller, *Fresh Expressions of Church*, Chapter 7.6.4.

27 Ibid., Chapter 7.3.4.

28 Ibid., Chapter 7.4.3.

29 Cray et al., *Mission-shaped Church*, p. vii.

30 Sabrina Müller, 'Fresh Expressions of Church' in *Handbuch für Kirchen-und Gemeindeentwicklung*, hg. von Ralph Kunz and Thomas Schlag, 1. Aufl. (Neukirchener Theologie, 2014), p. 453.

Messy Church and Sunday church in conversation

1 Herbert O'Driscoll, Bath and Wells Clergy Conference, Swanwick, September 1997.

2 Andrew Walls, *The Missionary Movement in Christian History* (T&T Clark, 1996), p. 7.

3 Rowan Williams, in Graham Cray and George Lings, *Mission-shaped Church: Church planting and fresh expressions of church in a changing context* (CHP, 2004/2009), p. vii.

4 (1) To proclaim the good news of the kingdom; (2) To teach, baptise and nurture new believers; (3) To respond to human need by loving service; (4) To seek to transform the unjust structures of society; (5) To strive to safeguard the integrity of creation and sustain and renew the earth. See www.anglicancommunion.org/identity/marks-of-mission.aspx.

5 See the chapter 'Messy Church and the sacraments' by Philip North, earlier in this book.

6 Lucy Moore, *Messy Church 2: Ideas for discipling a Christ-centred community* (BRF, 2008).

7 See the chapter 'Messy Church and the challenge of making disciples' by Stephen Kuhrt, later in this book.

8 See, for example, Fr Hywel Snook on Twitter (@fatherhywel), and the online pastor at https://onlinepastor.org.

9 See www.pray-as-you-go.org.

10 Paul Moore, *Making Disciples in Messy Church* (BRF, 2013), p. 104.

11 Tom Wright, *Restoring Hope in our Church* (video) (CTVC, 2003).

12 Judy Paulsen in George Lings (ed.), *Messy Church Theology* (BRF, 2013), pp. 68–90.

13 See the chapter 'Messy teamwork: developing the faith of team members' by Isabelle Hamley, earlier in this book.

14 'In 1960, 46% of the world's Christians were in Europe, with 7% in each of Asia and Africa. By 2010 it is estimated that these figures will be 22%, 18% and 17% respectively.' Peter Brierley, *Future Church: A global analysis of the Christian community to the year 2010* (Monarch, 1998), p. 37.

15 Peter Brierley, *Christian Research* (Eltham, 2000).

16   George Lings and Bob Hopkins, 'Mission-shaped Church: the Inside and Outside View', *Encounters on the Edge* 22 (Church Army, 2004), p. 4.

17   Cray and Lings, *Mission-shaped Church*, p. 40.

18   Interview with Margaret Withers, National Officer for Evangelism Amongst Children (Project REACH), 5 July 2005.

19   Bob Jackson in Lings (ed.), *Messy Church Theology*, p. 144.

20   Jackson in Lings (ed.), *Messy Church Theology*, p.146.

21   Lucy Moore, email conversation (1 April 2016).

Messy Church and play

1   Johan Huizinga, *Homo Ludens: A study of the play-element in culture* (Angelico Press, 2016).

2   Mihaly Csikszentmihalyi, *Beyond Boredom and Anxiety: Experiencing flow in work and play* (Wiley, 2000).

3   Jonah Lehrer, *Imagine: How creativity works* (Canongate, 2012).

4   James E. Loder, *The Transforming Moment* (Helmers & Howard, 1989).

5   Howard Gardner, *Frames of Mind: The theory of multiple intelligences* (Fontana, 1993).

6   Catherine Garvey, *Play (The Developing Child)* (Fontana, 1991).

7   Gabriel Moran, *Interplay: A theory of religion and education* (Christian Brothers, 1981).

8   James W. Fowler, *Stages of Faith: The psychology of human development and the quest for meaning* (Bravo, 1995).

9   Erik H. Erikson, *Childhood and Society* (Vintage, 1995).

10   Jerome W. Berryman, *The Spiritual Guidance of Children: Montessori, Godly Play, and the future* (Morehouse, 2013).

11   Jane Leadbetter, *Messy Prayer: Developing the prayer life of your Messy Church* (BRF, 2015).

12   flamecreativekids.blogspot.com.au/p/creative-prayer.html

The pastoral implications of Messy Church

1   See the chapter 'Messy teamwork: developing the faith of team members' by Isabelle Hamley, earlier in this book.

2   Bill Stone, 'CCPAS: Theology and safeguarding', www.ccpas.co.uk/about/theology.

3   www.churchofengland.org/clergy-office-holders/safeguarding-children-vulnerable-adults.aspx.

4 See Jim McManus, *Towards a Theology of Safeguarding* (2010): www. academia.edu/6003951/towards_a_theology_of_safeguarding.
5 Laurie Green, *Let's Do Theology: Resources for contextual theology* (Mowbray, 2009), p. 1.
6 Stephen B. Bevans, *Models of Contextual Theology* (Orbis, 2002), p. 37.
7 Declaration of Assent; preface in *Common Worship* (CHP, 2000), p. xi.
8 See www.acornchristian.org/listening/just-listen
9 Richard R. Osmer, *Practical Theology: An introduction* (Eerdmans, 2008).

Messy Church and evangelism

1 Lucy Moore, *Messy Church: Fresh ideas for building a Christ-centred community* (BRF, 2006), p. 21.
2 For an excellent overview of this, see Steve Hollinghurst, *Mission-Shaped Evangelism* (Canterbury Press, 2010), pp. 167–197.
3 Christopher J.H. Wright, *The Mission of God: Unlocking the Bible's grand narrative* (IVP, 2006), p. 23.
4 William J. Abraham, *The Logic of Evangelism* (Eerdmans, 1989), pp. 95, 101.
5 Lucy Moore, *Messy Hospitality* (BRF, 2016).
6 Such as George Lings (ed.), *Messy Church Theology* (BRF, 2013).
7 Paul Moore, *Making Disciples in Messy Church: Growing faith in an all-age community* (BRF, 2013), pp. 20–22.
8 Mark Ireland and Mike Booker, *Making New Disciples: Exploring the paradoxes of evangelism* (SPCK, 2015), p. 132.
9 Moore, *Making Disciples in Messy Church*, pp. 23–34.
10 Judy Paulsen, 'Does Messy Church make disciples?' in Lings (ed.), *Messy Church Theology*, pp. 72–74.
11 Ireland and Booker, *Making New Disciples*, p. 127.

Messy Church and the challenge of making disciples

1 See Stephen Kuhrt, *Church Growth through the Full Welcome of Children: The 'Sssh free church'* (Grove, 2009), pp. 6–7.
2 Vincent J. Donovan, *Christianity Rediscovered: An epistle from the Masai* (SCM, 2001), p. xix.
3 Andrew Davison and Alison Milbank, *For the Parish: A critique of Fresh Expressions* (SCM, 2010).
4 The word 'disciple' occurs only within the Gospels and Acts (264 times) rather than within Paul's letters. However, it is used here because the

calling to be a lifelong follower and learner of Jesus Christ pervades the whole of the New Testament.

5 See particularly Lucy Moore, *Messy Church 2: Ideas for discipling a Christ-centred community* (BRF, 2008) and Paul Moore, *Making Disciples in Messy Church* (BRF, 2013).

6 For a good introduction, see Michael B. Thompson, *The New Perspective on Paul* (Grove, 2002).

7 See the chapter 'Messy Church and the sacraments' by Philip North, earlier in this book.

8 See particularly N.T. Wright, *Justification: God's plan and Paul's vision* (SPCK, 2009).

9 See N.T. Wright, *Paul and the Faithfulness of God* (SPCK, 2013).

Missional structures for missional outcomes

1 While structures do not necessarily change things, they do provide plausibility contexts in which new thoughts or existing worldviews are changed or sustained; see James Sire, *Naming the Elephant: Worldview as a concept* (IVP, 2004), pp. 112–116. Apostolic leaders can generate, sustain and provide strategic direction for missional plausibility structures.

2 By this I am implying not just an era but a tone and sense of pioneering responsibility. See David Goodhew, Andrew Roberts and Michael Volland, *Fresh! An introduction to fresh expressions of church and pioneer ministry* (SCM, 2012), ch. 1.

3 I have previously briefly outlined this proposal in a footnote in my essay 'Missionary work in the Anglican Communion' in Ian Markham et al. (eds), *The Wiley-Blackwell Companion to the Anglican Communion* (Wiley-Blackwell, 2013), p. 684, ft. 7. On the rediscovery of the apostolic tradition of mission leadership, see William K. Kay, *Apostolic Networks in Britain: New ways of being church* (Paternoster, 2007) and Benjamin G. McNair-Scott, *Apostles Today: Making sense of contemporary charismatic apostolates* (Pickwick, 2004). For some recent thinking on modality and sodality, see the articles by George Lings, 'Why modality and sodality thinking is vital to understand future church' (www.churcharmy.org.uk/Publisher/File.aspx?ID=138339), and Mark Vanderverf, '"Mission shift" and the way forward' and 'The two structures of God's mission' in *Global Missiology* (April 2011). For reflections on how mission leadership relates to a life-world and a vision for a missional church, see Titre Ande, *Leadership and Authority: Bula Matrai and life-community ecclesiology*

in Congo (Regnum/CMS, 2010), especially ch. 6. On the importance of modality and sodality working together and in relation to church leadership, see Robert Blincoe, *A New Social Contract Relating Mission Societies to Ecclesiastical Structures* (William Carey, 2012).

4 See Tom Wright's summary, 'The challenge of the kingdom', in *The Challenge of Jesus* (SPCK, 2000), pp. 18–34.

5 This casts mission in neither the vertical nor the horizontal, but in the drama of history in which God is involved with creation and in which human involvement, enabled in the 'space' maintained by the Spirit, expresses the *telos* of mission as participating in the life of God as God participates in creation. See Ben Quash, *Theology and the Drama of History* (CUP, 2005).

6 See Tim Chester, *Mission and the Coming of God: Eschatology, the Trinity and mission in the theology of Moltmann and contemporary evangelicalism* (Paternoster, 2006). Quash and Chester's last chapters are worth comparing.

7 See David Hesselgrave and Ed Stetzer (eds), *Missionshift: Global mission issues in the third millennium* (Baker House, 2010) for an overview, in one tradition, of the changes taking place in the understandings of mission and the church.

8 For an overview of some movements which refreshed the church in mission, see a number of essays in John Walsh et al. (eds), *The Church of England, c.1689–1833: From toleration to tractarianism* (CUP, 1993). On refounding the church, see G.A. Arbuckle's many publications, such as *Refounding the Church: Dissent for leadership* (Chapman, 1993).

9 We have built on Ralph Winter's definition. In *The Two Structures of God's Redemptive Mission* (William Carey, 1974) he defines these terms as follows: 'a modality is a structured fellowship in which there is no distinction of sex or age, while a sodality is a structured fellowship in which membership involves an adult second decision beyond modality membership, and is limited by either age or sex or marital status. In this use of these terms, both the *denomination* and the *local congregation* are modalities, while a mission agency or a local men's club are sodalities. A secular parallel would be that of a town (modality) compared to a private business (a sodality)—perhaps a chain of stores found in many towns. The sodalities are subject to the authority of the more general structures, usually. They are "regulated" but not "administered" by the modalities.'

10 The most radical rethink of the doctrine of God from a missional perspective, drawing on recent mission thinking, can be found in John Flett, *The Witness of God: The Trinity, Missio Dei, Karl Barth and the nature*

of Christian community (Eerdmans, 2010). Christopher Wright explores the emergence of the word 'missional' in the opening chapter of *The Mission of God: Unlocking the Bible's grand narrative* (IVP, 2006). One helpful survey from the North American angle of the development of 'missional church' is found in Craig Van Gelder and Dwight J. Zscheile, *The Missional Church in Perspective: Mapping trends and shaping the conversation* (Baker, 2011). For another view, see Craig Ott et al., *Encountering Theology of Mission: Biblical foundations, historical developments, and contemporary issues* (Baker, 2010), ch. 8.

11 The revitalisation of Christianity as a non-Western and missional religion can be seen and charted in the writings of people like Kwame Bediako, *Theology and Identity: The impact of culture upon Christian thought in the second century and modern Africa* (Regnum, 1992); also *Christianity in Africa: The renewal of a non-Western religion* (Edinburgh University Press, 1995); and Vinoth Ramachandra, *The Recovery of Mission: Beyond the pluralist paradigm* (Paternoster, 1996).

12 See Andrew Walls, 'Origins of old northern and new southern Christianity' in *The Missionary Movement in Christian History: Studies in the transmission of the faith* (Orbis, 1996), pp. 68–79.

13 This has been recognised but will take time to mature. However, for explorations on the renewal of the church and revival movements, see *Fresh Expressions in the Mission of the Church* (CHP, 2012), ch. 6; Arthur Glasser, *Announcing the Kingdom: The story of God's mission in the Bible* (Baker, 2003), ch. 19; Howard Snyder, *Models of Church and Mission: A survey*, Center for the Study of World Christian Revitalization Movements, © 2010 Howard A. Snyder—Tyndale Seminary; George Pierce, *Revitalization of a Sodality* (unpublished MTh thesis in missiology, Fuller University, 1987). On missiology, in the 'Gospel and our culture' tradition inspired by Lesslie Newbigin, see Wilbert Shenk's essay, 'A missiology of Western culture: background and development of a project' in John Corrie and Cathy Ross (eds), *Mission in Context: Explorations inspired by J. Andrew Kirk* (Ashgate, 2012), pp. 169–187. For an exploration of what this might require, see David Kettle, *Western Culture in Gospel Context* (Cascade, 2011); and for a similar take but from a global perspective, see Mark Laing, *From Crisis to Creation: Lesslie Newbigin and the reinvention of Christian mission* (Pickwick, 2012). There are many other resources for developing a new missiological perspective, but a most stimulating new read is Timothy Tennent, *Invitation to World Missions: A trinitarian missiology for the twenty-first century* (Kregel, 2010).

14 *Mission-shaped Church: Church planting and fresh expressions of church in a changing context* (CHP, 2004/2009).

15 Philip Richter and Leslie Francis, in *Gone but Not Forgotten* (DLT, 1998), describe English society as being made up of regular church attenders (10%), fringe attenders (10%), closed de-churched (20%), open de-churched (20%) and non-churched (40%).

16 'Growing, maturing, ripening: what might an older Messy Church look like?' in George Lings, *Messy Church Theology: Exploring the significance of Messy Church for the wider church* (BRF, 2013), p. 242.

17 George Lings, 'What is the DNA of Messy Church?' in Lings, *Messy Church Theology*, pp. 156–158 (see the double-helix diagram on p. 157).

18 Lings, *Messy Church Theology*, pp. 252–254.

19 Andrew Walls, *The Missionary Movement in Christian History* (T&T Clark, 1996), p. 258.

20 The seven stages are before Pentecost (Acts 1); after Pentecost (Acts 2—5); Stephen (Acts 6—7); Samaria and the Ethiopian eunuch (Acts 8); Cornelius and his household (Acts 10—11:18); Antioch (11:19–26); and mission to the Gentiles (Acts 12—28). See Roger Schroeder and Stephen B. Bevans, *Constants in Context: A theology of mission for today* (Orbis, 2004), p. 13. This book has now become essential reading, along with David J. Bosch's classic, *Transforming Mission: Paradigm shifts in theology of mission* (Orbis, 2011). Other significant recent books on missiology include Michael Goheen, *Introducing Christian Mission Today: Scripture, history and issues* (IVP, 2014) and Scott Sunquist, *Understanding Christian Mission: Participation in suffering and glory* (Baker, 2013).

21 Here, I would emphasise the role of nodality (particularly its episcopal version) in leading Christian mission engagement. For example, Rowan Williams notes the varying challenges of episcopal leadership: 'Western Christendom had its common ground in the Latin tongue and the authority of the Curia; eastern Orthodoxy in the political ambience of the Imperial Court, and a kind of Byzantine political-ideological-aesthetic vernacular; non-Chalcedonian Christianity… in the common social situation of a religio-ethnic minority under Muslim rule. Within these circles, the bishop's interpretive work does not involve the demanding cross-cultural translations of a more pluralist situation. But in the latter kind of situation, the bishop's unifying authority within a community will depend in large measure on his sensitivity to the range of Christian options in the world at large, and thus upon his interpretative skills in this wider context. Hence the need for structures which permit precisely this kind of exchange, and which nurture and preserve a "catholic"

perspective in the bishop's mind, enabling him, *inter alia*, to speak more clearly and powerfully on behalf of strangers and minorities within his own community.' ('Authority and the Bishop in the Church' in Mark Santer (ed.), *Their Lord and Ours*, SPCK, 1982, p. 102.)

22 Craig Van Gelder, *Local and Mobile: A study of two functions*, privately distributed, 1975.

23 However, there is a distinction, as Arthur Burns notes in his essay, 'English "church reform" revisited, 1780–1840' in A. Burns and J. Innes (eds), *Rethinking the Age of Reform* (CUP, 2003), pp. 136–162. The term 'church reform' is not applied to the kind of major changes in the church which reflected the reforms in wider society, and the term is never applied to mission. The transformation, the reform, of the polity of the Church of England by mission is one still taking place—as proposed here—and hastened now by the kind of social pressures, such as globalisation, which created the diocesan renewal of which Burns writes (see above). On these earlier changes, see his *The Diocesan Revival in the Church of England c.1800–1870* (OUP, 1999).

24 Here I'm drawing on Andrew Walls' thought. First, in his essay 'A history of the expansion of Christianity reconsidered' (in *The Cross-Cultural Process in Christian History*, T&T Clark, 2002, pp. 18–25), Walls, reflecting Latourette's work, considers ways of testing whether Christian expansion is genuine. The third test, the gospel test, is the one I believe is the nodality test: has the gospel impacted on humanity as a whole? This is the 'Why?' of mission, and tests the purpose of Christian expansion. Second, in 'The gospel as prisoner and liberator' (in *The Missionary Movement in Christian History*, T&T Clark, 1996, pp. 3–16), Walls explores both the pilgrimage and indigenisation principles and shows how both are necessary. I am suggesting that these are the sodality and modality dimensions which, when combined in the reshaping of the church's life, lead to a vitality in Christian expansion (what Walls would call, following Latourette, the breadth and depth).

25 For one of the most extensive discussions of this view, see Paul Peirson, *The Dynamics of Christian Mission: History through a missiological perspective* (William Carey, 2009).

26 Karl Barth bemoans the 'yawning gap' in Reformation churches—a goal which transcends the church, something that cross-cultural mission stimulates and requires. See Waldron Scott, *Karl Barth's Theology of Mission* (IVP, 1978), p. 22.

27 In a series of articles Robert Blincoe considers the ongoing existence of the two structures, their denominational character and the mutual

benefit that both structures can be to each other. See three editions of the *International Journal of Frontier Missions*, 2002: 19.1, pp. 5–8; 19.2, pp. 5–9; and 19.3, pp. 43–46. What is proposed in this chapter is a symbiosis at diocesan and provincial levels within a denominational tradition but drawing on a reimagining of missional leadership in the apostolic tradition.

28 Ralph Winter identifies nine characteristics of mission societies: 1. Voluntary, deeper commitment; 2. Response to a challenge; 3. Stress on both devotion and active involvement; 4. Task forces ready for any good work; 5. An organisational esprit de corps; 6. Both come-structures and go-structures; 7. Amazing durability (of purpose and existence); 8. Stress on Christian basics; 9. Normative patterns of discipline— for example, a community of members, related to church structure but semi-autonomous, with a structure of authority (quasi-familial), common property, celibate chastity or monosexual membership, and elite commitment beyond that of ordinary church members. ('Protestant mission societies: the American experience', *Missiology: An international review*, Vol. VII, No. 2, April 1979, pp. 163–164.)

29 See Craig Van Gelder, *Local and Mobile: A study of two functions*, reformatted with permission, 2015, pp. 13–23. I would argue that the apostolic dynamic is grounded in Christ himself and this ministry should be incorporated into the nature of the church through the office of bishop and senior leadership. See the Church of England's report from the Faith and Order Commission on Senior Leadership (CHP: 2015), particularly the section on Episcopacy, pp. 52–57.

30 There is a vast amount of literature on episcopacy (see Paul Avis, *Becoming a Bishop* (T&T Clark, 2015). I am not implying that episcopacy solves everything or that my interpretation is *the* Anglican one. In *Anglican Theology* (T&T Clark, 2012), Mark Chapman says that Anglicans expect disagreements to be resolved by bishops, but can't agree on what episcopal authority is!

31 In Winchester Diocese we are developing a scheme whereby we can provide both modal and sodal structures operating collaboratively within the oversight of the bishop and diocesan governance.

32 See Arbuckle, *Refounding the Church*, chs 4 and 5.

33 See Sam Metcalf's review of Robert Clinton's understanding of apostolic leadership in *Beyond the Local Church: How apostolic movements can change the world* (IVP, 1995), pp. 92–95.

34 *Royal Priesthood: A theology of ministry* (T&T Clark, 1993), ch. 5.

35 See note 1 above. The three types are the canonical founders (equivalent to the early apostles); coordinating hierarchy (supports all ministries in local churches); and corporate and shared (apostolic functions move between church members in relation to context and demand). See also the Faith and Order Commission report *Recognition of Orders* (February 2014), pp. 5–7.

36 There's much that resonates with the approach to episcope outlined by Steven Croft, *Ministry in Three Dimensions: Ordination and leadership in the local church* (DLT, 1997), pp. 139–192.

37 Adapted from the latest version of the research carried out by George Lings and others on behalf of the Church of England; and summarised in 'What is an Anglican fresh expression of Church? Ten criteria' (Church Army Research Unit, June 2014).

38 This is the classic three-self model developed by Henry Venn of CMS for encouraging indigenisation/contextualisation in cross-cultural church planting, and further developed to include the fourth self: self-theologising. (See Richard Trull, *The Fourth Self: Theological education to facilitate self-theologising for local church leaders in Kenya*, Lang, 2013.)

39 It is also clear that a Messy Church approach can be adapted for sodal church. For example, the newly 'acknowledged community' of Hope-weavers has elements of the Messy Church approach—particularly the five senses approach to prayer; nevertheless, Hopeweavers has its own charism with a distinctive focus for its outreach and its community life.

40 Here I'm referring not just to the entrepreneurial leadership of sodal ministry, but to the apostolic leadership that sees the significance of combining modality and sodality in a collaborative effort. I'm taking forward proposals like those of Metcalf in his *Beyond the Local Church* by combining it with movements like 'The Externally Focused Church'—for example, Eric Swanson and Rick Rusaw, *The Externally Focused Quest: Becoming the best church for the community* (Wiley, 2010).

41 Graham Cray's *Disciples and Citizens: A vision for distinctive living* (IVP, 2007) explores this wider context.

42 *Messy Church: Fresh ideas for building a Christ-centred community* (BRF, 2006); *Messy Church 2: Ideas for discipling a Christ-centred community* (BRF, 2008); and *Messy Church 3: Fifteen sessions for exploring the Christian life with families* (BRF, 2012).

43 What is proposed here builds on the insights of Paul Moore in *Making Disciples in Messy Church* (BRF, 2013) in which he considers how disciples learn together over time, and through different kinds of learning, how to be disciples together so that they can be disciples in the wider

world. The development of the kind of practice which supports this—the wisdom found in practising knowledge—can be seen in Benjamin T. Conner, *Practicing Witness: A missional vision of Christian practices* (Eerdmans, 2011) and *Amplifying Our Witness: Giving voice to adolescents with development disabilities* (Eerdmans, 2012); see also Andrew Root, *Christopraxis: A practical theology of the cross* (Fortress, 2014).

44 Nigel Rooms has suggested seven characteristics of English culture or Christianity—moderation, humorous moaning, privacy, fair play, class, courtesy, pragmatism. See *The Faith of the English: Integrating Christ and culture* (SPCK, 2011), pp. 44–54.

45 'Business as mission' is now common in mission literature, but the connections between 'business as mission', common good, vocation and social economics are still emerging. Having a holistic view of mission is a crucial first step but connecting it to work is then also required. See R.W. Alexander, *Profession-als: Men and women partnering with the Trinity in everyday life* (CreateSpace, 2001). For two overviews of business as mission, see C. Neal Johnson, *Business as Mission: A comprehensive guide to theory and practice* (IVP, 2009) and Tom Steffan and Mike Barnett (eds), *Business as Mission: From impoverished to empowered* (William Care, 2006).

46 Martin Nkafu Nkemnkia, *African Vitalogy: A step forward in African thinking* (Paulines, 1999), p. 11.

47 On the gospel and culture debate, see note 6. The challenge is to go back and do some more thorough strategic work, questioning a model of inculturation as contextualisation or the use of the reflective cycle as tactic. For example, Alan Thomson, *Culture in a Post-Secular Context: Theological possibilities in Milbank, Barth and Bediako* (Pickwick, 2014).

48 For a take on the five marks of mission from younger theologians from around the world, see Cathy Ross (ed.), *Life-Widening Mission: Global Anglican perspectives* (Regnum, 2012).

49 See Andrew Walls and Cathy Ross (eds), *Mission in the 21st Century: Exploring five marks of global mission* (DLT, 2008) for lots of reflections on the significance of this kind of witness.

50 One of the early accessible attempts to grapple with this global change and cultural challenge can be found in Martin Robinson, *To Win the West* (Bible Society/CPAS), 1996.

51 See Michael Moynagh's book and his appreciation of Messy Church: *Being Church, Doing Life: Creating gospel communities where life happens* (Lion Hudson, 2014), pp. 102–104, 182–184.

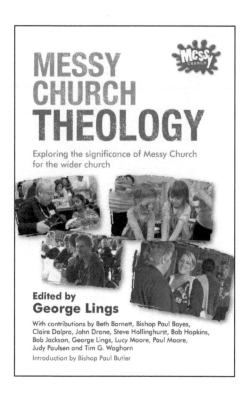

Messy Church Theology is the first title to encapsulate the theology of Messy Church. Through chapters by contributors from a variety of church and academic backgrounds and case studies by Messy Church practitioners, it gathers together some of the discussions around Messy Church and assesses the impact of this ministry, placing it in the context of wider developments within the church community.

Messy Church Theology
Exploring the significance of Messy Church for the wider church
Edited by George Lings
978 0 85746 171 1 £9.99

brfonline.org.uk

A challenging question for Messy Church leaders is, 'Can Messy Church nurture new faith and make converts into disciples?' This book analyses how families are journeying to faith through Messy Church and how we can support them. It explores what we mean by discipleship, and methods for making disciples, from scripture and church tradition. The aim is to encourage ministers and lay leaders to see how their Messy Church can be an intentional disciple-making community.

Making Disciples in Messy Church
Growing faith in an all-age community
Paul Moore
978 0 85746 218 3 £6.99

brfonline.org.uk

BRF

Transforming
lives and communities

Christian growth and understanding of the Bible

Resourcing individuals, groups and leaders in churches for their own spiritual journey and for their ministry

Church outreach in the local community

Offering three programmes that churches are embracing to great effect as they seek to engage with their local communities and transform lives

Teaching Christianity in primary schools

Working with children and teachers to explore Christianity creatively and confidently

Children's and family ministry

Working with churches and families to explore Christianity creatively and bring the Bible alive

Visit **brf.org.uk** for more information on BRF's work
Review this book on Twitter using **#BRFconnect**

brf.org.uk

The Bible Reading Fellowship (BRF) is a Registered Charity (No. 233280)